"In our postmodern age, it's all the more important that Christians cultivate ancient friendships, apprenticing with broken and beautiful saints who've preceded us. Their lives of devotion, service, and sacrifice help us to reimagine our own. In this wise, humble, passionate book, Karen Marsh invites you to meet the ancient friends who have nourished her faith. It's a joyful, honest journey that will make you want to join this pilgrimage for yourself."

James K. A. Smith, Calvin College, author of *You Are What You Love*

"Sit down and pour yourself a glass of Karen Wright Marsh's *Vintage Saints and Sinners*. At first sip, you are transported into delightful stories of Christians past. As you drink more deeply, *Vintage Saints and Sinners* engages difficult issues of faith, doubts and loves, wisdom, and the practice of justice in the world. This is a gracious book full of charming prose and profound truths with just the right complexity of spiritual insight for everyday life. Taste and see!"

Diana Butler Bass, author of *Grounded: Finding God in the World—A Spiritual Revolution*

"There are many times when Christian ministry—particularly activist ministries that pursue the full expression of the kingdom of God in the world—can be an arduous and lonely task. It can feel like we are the first ones to tread this territory. Karen Marsh looks back upon an important spiritual history. She offers important examples and role models who remind us that we are never alone when we pursue the fullness of the kingdom of God. If every activist Christian were to engage in a daily reading of this text and actually put into practice what is offered by these vintage Christians, Christianity could actually serve a healthier witness to the kingdom of God."

Soong-Chan Rah, Milton B. Engebretson Professor of Church Growth and Evangelism, North Park Theological Seminary, author of *The Next Evangelicalism* and *Prophetic Lament*

"The winsome brilliance of Karen Wright Marsh's ability to encapsulate gorgeous little vignettes of history's greatest contemplative mystics and fierce justice advocates makes *Vintage Saints and Sinners* a timely work. From the most spectacular to the uttermost undramatic conversions, each hero and shero Karen introduces highlights an embodied example of vocational fidelity that is both inspiring and inviting."

Christopher L. Heuertz, cofounder of Gravity, a Center for Contemplative Activism, author of *The Sacred Enneagram*

"Righteousness, we know, is endlessly complicated. In *Vintage Saints and Sinners*, Karen Marsh shows that it's also a living process, a communal drama of joy and liveliness into which we're invited. With wit, care, and deep lyricism, Karen helps us to see that saints—who are also always sinners—are on our side. Where we are, they've already been. We get to meet their messy witness with our own. One day at a time."

David Dark, author of *Life's Too Short to Pretend You're Not Religious*

"It's not hard to imagine being drawn into a good conversation about things that matter with Karen Marsh. At the same time playful and profound, with heart and mind she invites us in, opening her deep, rich reading of the 'sainted ones' of the centuries, making them be what they must be: ordinary men and women who lived lives near to God—with every possible heartache and hope. But that's the good gift of this book: it makes these saints be sinners like us, people who long for honest faith, honest hope, and honest love. *Vintage Saints and Sinners* is a book for the everyman and everywoman, pilgrims across the centuries that we are."

Steven Garber, principal of the Washington Institute for Faith, Vocation & Culture, author of *Visions of Vocation*

"This page-turning pilgrimage journal offers readers way-bread from—and for—the fallible and glorious communion of quotidian saints."

Susan R. Holman, author of *Beholden*

"There are few things in this world that more ably transform us than our encounters with real stories. Stories that tell of joy and shame. Of hope and anguish. Of the very hard work that leads to a world of goodness, beauty, and redemption—but not without the honest rendition of all the stumbling in the dark that necessarily accompanies such godly liberation. These are the stories that we so desperately need to hear, and they are the very stories that Karen Marsh has so thoughtfully given us with *Vintage Saints and Sinners*. Stories not only of the saints of clay feet who we all know about, but also the story that is her own, the one that ties all the others—the reader's not the least—into the grand narrative into which God is writing all who are willing to be included. If you want your hope to be strengthened, if you want your mind to be renewed, and if you want your story to be changed, look no further: this collection of stories is for you."

Curt Thompson, author of *The Soul of Shame*

VINTAGE Saints *AND* Sinners

25 CHRISTIANS WHO TRANSFORMED MY FAITH

KAREN WRIGHT MARSH

FOREWORD BY LAUREN WINNER

An imprint of InterVarsity Press
Downers Grove, Illinois

InterVarsity Press
P.O. Box 1400, Downers Grove, IL 60515-1426
ivpress.com
email@ivpress.com

InterVarsity Press® is the book-publishing division of InterVarsity Christian Fellowship/USA®, a movement of students and faculty active on campus at hundreds of universities, colleges, and schools of nursing in the United States of America, and a member movement of the International Fellowship of Evangelical Students. For information about local and regional activities, visit intervarsity.org.

While any stories in this book are true, some names and identifying information may have been changed to protect the privacy of individuals.

Cover design: Cindy Kiple
Interior design: Jeanna Wiggins
Images: Cretan man: Cretan Man by Manolis Grigoreas, Private Collection / Malva Gallery / Bridgeman Images
lady with cat: Young Lady with Cat by Manolis Grigoreas, Private Collection / Malva Gallery / Bridgeman Images
Saint George: Saint George by Manolis Grigoreas, Private Collection / Malva Gallery / Bridgeman Images
Saint Paraskevi: Saint Paraskevi by Manolis Grigoreas, Private Collection / Malva Gallery / Bridgeman Images

ISBN 978-0-8308-4496-8 (paperback)
ISBN 978-0-8308-4513-2 (hardcover)
ISBN 978-0-8308-9237-2 (digital)

Printed in the United States of America ♾

Library of Congress Cataloging-in-Publication Data
Names: Marsh, Karen Wright, 1961- author.
Title: Vintage saints and sinners : 25 Christians who transformed my faith / Karen Wright Marsh.
Description: Downers Grove : InterVarsity Press, 2017. | Includes bibliographical references.
Identifiers: LCCN 2017038100 (print) | LCCN 2017033889 (ebook) | ISBN 9780830892372 (eBook) | ISBN 9780830845132 (hardcover : alk. paper)
Subjects: LCSH: Christian biography.
Classification: LCC BR1700.3 (print) | LCC BR1700.3 .M37 2017 (ebook) | DDC 270.092/2 [B] — dc23
LC record available at https://lccn.loc.gov/2017038100

P 25 24 23 22 21 20 19 18 17 16 15 14 13 12 11 10 9 8 7 6 5 4 3 2
Y 43 42 41 40 39 38 37 36 35 34 33 32 31 30 29 28 27 26 25

for

Charles

Henry, Will, *and* Nan

the dearest of companions

God creates out of nothing.

Wonderful! you say.

Yes, to be sure.

But God does what is still more wonderful:

God makes saints out of sinners.

Søren Kierkegaard

❧ ❧ ❧

Contents

Foreword

Lauren Winner

How does one go about living a Christian life?

That's the question *Vintage Saints and Sinners* addresses. Its answer can be boiled down to four slightly technical words: moral theology is hagiography. Put differently, the question of how to live a Christian life isn't answered by a list of do's and don'ts. It's answered by looking at lives that have been lived in response to Jesus.

I found myself pondering a few questions as I read this book. First, I noticed, quite simply, that lives lived in response to Jesus look very varied. Yet I wondered: Do the lives of Brother Lawrence and Sophie Scholl and C. S. Lewis, varied as they are, have anything in common? When we look at lives lived in response to Jesus, are there shapes that frequently recur? It seemed to me as I read, for example, that lives lived in response to Jesus are also perforce lived in peculiar relationship to the world. If you live in response to Jesus, the world will look different to you than it looks to your neighbors who, instead of attending to Jesus, pass their days in attention to the stock market, the *New Yorker*, or the devil. If you live in response to Jesus, you'll look out your window and see a world created by God. You'll see the powerless crucified by the powerful, and you'll see the crucified One rising, and because you see those things—because you see the world with an eye attuned to Jesus—you'll organize your life differently than your neighbor whose eye is attuned to the Dow Jones. Because they see differently and respond to what they see, saints often flout local convention and violate local norms. They often scandalize and unsettle. Sometimes they get arrested and killed.

In part because saints live in weird relation to the world, inviting the saints into your life can be tricky. Indeed, reading about a saint can occasionally induce despair. I read about the heroism of Sophie Scholl, and the demons who accompany me on my daily rounds perk up and say, "If the standard is staring down Hitler and being guillotined on treason charges, why not admit that you're not really trying to live like Jesus at all? You can't even consistently remember to bring canned goods to church on the first Sunday of the month." And then the demons are off to the races, explaining that I'm a pathetic excuse for a Christian and suggesting that instead of praying Evening Prayer, I rewatch the second season of *House of Cards*.

Here's the thing to say to those demons (I manage to say it about one-third of the time): *I don't read about the saints in order to imitate them. I read about the saints because they show me something about myself.* To be frank, I don't really want to live like Francis of Assisi or Mother Teresa. But I do want to ask those saints to help me look at my life through the prism of theirs. Aelred of Rievaulx, a twelfth-century monk who wrote an enduring treatise about friendship, does not inspire me to join a monastery, but he can help me see what kind of a friend I am. Brother Lawrence, a seventeenth-century monk, learned, through years of serving in his monastery's kitchen, to "do little things for God; I turn the cake that is frying on the pan for love of him." He can help me see how Jesus is transfiguring the ordinary mundanities of my own life.

As you read *Vintage Saints and Sinners*, notice which saints especially hold your attention. Not all of them will. You might particularly connect with one saint, or maybe two. (Notice, also, which saints particularly repel you; the Holy Spirit might be using your discomfort to draw your attention to something you need to see.) I suspect that over our lives, each of us is given two or three or four saints with whom to live in particular intimacy. Your three or four will be different from mine because you're gifted in ways I'm not, and because you're damaged in ways I'm not. Which saints is God offering you, to help illumine and burnish your particular gifts, and to help illumine and heal your particular damages?

This is a book about people, but it's also about God. It's about God because when you carefully consider anything—a virus, a chocolate layer cake, a sparrow—you'll ultimately see something about the way that thing participates in its Creator. That's true of cakes and sparrows, but it might be especially true of people. People are created in God's image, so when I study a person whose life is fully responsive to Jesus, I see what it's like for an image and likeness of God to be in a world like this one. Take Francis of Assisi, who gave away almost all he owned—he was, as *Vintage Saints and Sinners* puts it, "liberated from possessions." The picture of Francis giving away money, books, clothing, sandals shows me something about my own life—it sets in clear relief my intense possessiveness, and my unreliable spurts of giving things away. But it also shows me something about the God in whom Francis participates: Francis's life shows me that God is One who responds to a world in which things can be owned by undercutting and removing the possibility of ownership. Because the lives of Francis and Mother Teresa and Sophie Scholl are lives taken into Jesus, they show us something about Jesus himself.

There are twenty-five saints whose stories are told here, but there is a twenty-sixth saint lurking in these pages: the book's author, Karen Marsh, whose saintly charisms include allowing the saints to season her soul. In testifying about the saints, Karen is taking up a well-established bit of Christian choreography. In every generation, there are Christians who have allowed themselves to be especially worked over by the saints, and who are called to introduce the saints to the rest of us. (The conversion of one so great as Augustine was prompted by one friend's description of two other friends being converted by reading the life of St. Antony. In other words, even a decidedly circuitous witness to saintly influence can be efficacious.) Karen's charism is a fabulism of sorts; in *Vintage Saints and Sinners*, she's worked a kind of magical realism in which the faithful of the ages are able to walk right into our own haphazardly faithful, twenty-first-century lives. And of course, there's a twenty-seventh saint here, too, or at least a twenty-seventh saint-in-the-making—the reader. You.

May *Vintage Saints and Sinners* help you find saintly companions, and may it thereby show you something about how your particular life can be lived in response to the One who created, redeemed, and sustains you.

Introduction

Notes from the Crossroads

A Christian is one who is on the way,
though not necessarily very far along it,
and who has at least some dim and
half-baked idea of whom to thank.

Frederick Buechner

I grew up on Sunday school tales of godly Christians who made the grand gesture, brave missionaries like William Carey who sailed from England to India, undaunted by the perils, exhorting, "Expect great things from God! Attempt great things for God!" Look into my kindergarten journal and you'll read: "What I Want to Be: A Missionary Nurse in Africa." I would bandage wounds from lion attacks and fearlessly preach salvation; that was the future for me.

By the time I declared a philosophy major in college, dreams of a trailblazing medical career were replaced by romantic visions of the contemplative lives of Thérèse of Lisieux and Scholastica. I was intrigued by the idea of a nun's cloistered existence, with its peaceful rhythm of ethereal Gregorian chants sung in a sunlit chapel, abundant alone time for reading in a private cell, and suppers of freshly baked bread and artisanal cheeses savored around a distressed oak table. But as a Presbyterian minister's daughter, the convent was never more than a vague notion I'd picked up from the *Sound of Music*.

Heroic exploits and ecstatic revelations rarely feature in my life these days. Instead, my heart wanders—sometimes caught in distraction, fear, and doubt, and at other times reaching for confidence, constancy and hope. Never a nurse nor a full-time holy woman, I have found instead that my career has taken a winding path to Theological Horizons, the nonprofit ministry I direct, centered at the Bonhoeffer House near the campus of the University of Virginia, where I teach, feed and mentor college students, and host scholars and community members. My family—my husband, Charles, a UVA professor, and our three millennial children, Henry, Will, and Nan—keep me firmly grounded in what Kathleen Norris calls "the quotidian mysteries." Every morning begins a new episode on a journey without maps.

Throughout my life, as I've become a mother and not a nun, a teacher and not a missionary, I've been accompanied by "vintage" Christians—spiritual mentors from across the Christian tradition, committed Jesus followers who kept the faith in their own times and places. What began as an intellectual study, even idealized admiration, of notable spiritual figures has become a deeper personal experience of reading from the heart. Over the years, I have been awed by ancient lives of humility and strength. Even now, sitting in my living room, I discover more of my own unexpected connections to obscure believers from distant eras. They light up my imagination, calling me to greater things, even as the kitchen sink fills with sticky plates, tax deadlines arrive, and I forget to pray.

While scrubbing pots and pans in the kitchen of a seventeenth-century French monastery, Brother Lawrence learned to practice the comforting presence of God. When I know that, though frustrated by failure, he persisted in his spiritual disciplines year after year, I see how callously impatient I am for the rush of a spiritual high. Then I meet Amanda Berry Smith, a woman who, though she was born in slavery, prayed her way through trembling fear to preach of God's power to white Americans and evangelize throughout four far-flung continents. Each vintage Christian, whatever the century, encountered God for themselves and each responded wholeheartedly. To learn their stories is to see my own time-bound experience in the light of God's pursuing presence. They bring me perspective, calm, and the hope that I too will come to bear the marks of a vibrant spiritual life.

I've read the words of radically committed Christians—and they seem, at first, to be more righteously determined than I could ever be. No wonder: the historical, faithful people you and I often speak of as "saints" are models of extraordinary conviction and intimidating courage. There are the ones who've been canonized by the Roman Catholic Church, recognized by the eternal honorific "Saint" in front of their names. Others lived such godly lives that we can't help but envision them on pedestals. That kind of veneration prompted Dorothy Day, tireless advocate for the poor, to say, "Don't call me a saint. I don't want to be dismissed so easily."

As I've gotten up close to the personal stories of vintage Christians, I have met them in their humanity. They may be called saints, but they are sinners, strugglers, and seekers too. When they speak across the centuries, their lives turn out to be just as messy as (and sometimes much messier than) mine. I've learned that the smiling Mother Teresa, serving the dying poor in Calcutta, felt for years that her desperate prayers were met by God's silence. And that the eminent intellectual defender of the faith, C. S. Lewis, went through his teens and twenties convinced that Christianity was for idiots.

I've moved beyond seeing these people as inaccessible super-saints and have encountered them as perfect companions for a real-life pilgrimage. They are wise guides in the faith who have been this way before. Older brothers and sisters who urge me on, reassuring me with their own tales of travail and discovery.

When I find myself wandering, at a loss, through a foreign city street, or gritting my teeth over an unwelcome bill in the morning mail, their reassuring words come to me. They are not shocked when I snap at my children or take my husband for granted. In better times, they remind me that it is God who gives a leisurely hour to sleep in the warm sun or sit in silence with a close friend. Whether in anxious, frustrated, lonely moments or in restful, joyous celebrations, these saints and sinners know how I feel.

Am I a paragon of faith? (The honest answer is no.) While I once thought that I should labor to look and act and believe just like the other "successful" Christians in my life, I've been freed up by something Thomas Merton once wrote: "For me to be a saint means to be myself." Not that godly person I greatly admire, but *myself*. I see now that I'm engaged in a creative, enlivening, one-of-a-kind work of God in me, redeemed by Christ for good things. Who knows what kind of saint I, as myself, am becoming?

From these vintage saints and sinners, in all of their variety, I am learning lessons about the qualities of authentic spirituality—about faith as a journey through struggles and weakness and into freedom and true strength. I find that Julian of Norwich had hopes that are much like mine, that Martin Luther wrestled with anxiety, and that Benedict's teaching brings a healthier rhythm to every day. I accompany very human exemplars in the faith who cheer me on with profound yet approachable wisdom.

This book is a journal from my spiritual pilgrimage: scribbled confessions, quick descriptions of the quirky people I've met along the way, incomplete reflections on how I'm trying to make sense of it all. You won't find twenty-five complete biographies here; let's leave those to the historians. Instead, it's my hope that by telling you some tales from the lives of vintage Christians—with their struggles, joys and revelations—and by opening up about the lessons I've learned, you'll discover that God's saving, guiding, transforming grace is here for you, as well.

PART 1

Asking

Stand at the crossroads and look;
ask for the ancient paths,
ask where the good way is, and walk in it,
and you will find rest for your souls.

Jeremiah 6:16

SØREN KIERKEGAARD 1813–1855

Take a Long Walk

The best help in all action is to pray—

that is true genius; then one never goes wrong.

AT OUR HOUSE, THE NEW YEAR ARRIVES IN AUGUST. Fresh beginnings and great expectations: a new semester in Charlottesville. This morning, Nan is out the door to high school. My husband, Charles, scrambles to print a university course syllabus. I glance at my Google calendar; the coming months are already mapped out in busy blocks of color. Goodbye, lazy summer.

Three hours from now, sixty undergrads will walk through the Bonhoeffer House door, each one hungry for the homemade lunch that's become a Friday tradition here. Guess who's cooking? Before I start the lasagna, I require strong coffee. In the few seconds it takes to grind the beans, I stand still and rehearse Søren Kierkegaard's prayer, "Teach me, O God, not to make a martyr of myself through stifling reflection. Teach me to breathe deeply in faith." And I take one full breath. In and out.

The moment passes and I'm off again, energized by action, to-do lists, everyday projects. Usually, momentum is enough to keep me buzzing through the day. Lately, though, I've felt a tug in my chest, a twist of uneasiness below the surface of things. I've been drawn back to my battered 1956 copy of *The Prayers of Kierkegaard*. I'm slow to admit what so many believers already know well: time in prayer, time with God, is my only hope for peace. Prayer brings life, if only I will choose it.

❧ ❧ ❧

Søren Kierkegaard did not make his name on the merits of a dynamic public prayer life. In his own time, the existentialist philosopher rambled for hours through the charming streets and hidden passages of Copenhagen, stopping to talk with random folks along the way. Everyone in town recognized Søren, the spindly, comical figure whose tousled hair stuck up nearly six inches from his forehead.

Søren's brilliant, caustic wit was admired all over. You wouldn't have guessed that behind the roving, familiar figure with top hat and walking cane there was a melancholy guy trying to know and solve the deep riddle of life. He held a whole lot inside, determined to understand himself before he could know anything else—and that included God.

Even as an outwardly vivacious youngster, Søren always kept his true feelings concealed. When he wrote of his childhood later, he described himself as an intense boy in the power of a "monstrously brooding temperament," a child who played a pitiful game: to keep everyone from guessing how secretly unhappy he really was. But it was no picnic to be the youngest of Michael Kierkegaard's seven children. Søren's haunted, pietistic father was convinced that their family was cursed. Michael gloomily predicted that all of his children would die tragically by thirty-three, Jesus' age at his crucifixion. Old man Kierkegaard took his kids on treks to the cemetery where he exhorted them to dwell on the agonies of Christ and meditate on their own horrific sins. No wonder little Søren was filled with dread.

As he grew older, teenaged Søren was both repelled by and attracted to his father's fierce religion. He wrestled with faith as a theology student at the University of Copenhagen. As Søren began thinking for himself, the weighty old orthodox Christian dogma cracked and shifted. What options were left to him then? Punishing, wrathful

Avenger or respectable, distant Deity—could either God be true? And what did any divine being have to do with him and his small life? Søren looked to philosophy as a way to slip the snares of religion.

I've always liked philosophy. Ancient Greeks pondering the nature of reality. German idealists and French postmodernists. Logic, with its axioms and arguments. Thought experiments to sharpen my mind. In fact, Aristotle's words are posted over my desk: "It is the mark of an educated mind to be able to entertain a thought without accepting it." I don't exactly stay up at night worrying over concepts, but I do enjoy philosophy for the healthy intellectual workout.

Søren took philosophizing far more to heart; his was a high-stakes search. Stalking the alleys of Copenhagen, occupied by interior puzzling, Kierkegaard was plagued by the personal problem of purpose. In the pages of his journal, Søren wrote, "What I really lack is to be clear in my mind what I am to *do*, not what I am to *know*." He was after an intellectual understanding that would enliven his existence in the world—one grand passion to comprehend his essential self, to know truth that was true for him, to find the idea for which he could live and die.

Søren's melancholy deepened as philosophy failed to bear the weight of his all-encompassing quest for meaning. Still, he struggled on, hoping it wouldn't prove to be to be a dead end. As for theology, Søren couldn't shake his suspicion that beyond abstract religious dogma there actually was a divine reality: the person of Jesus who would demand a startling commitment. But at the unwelcome prospect of a full spiritual conversion that would surely offend his reason and clash with his emotions, Søren determined to try everything else before he became "seriously a Christian." If Jesus held a radical cure, it was a not a medicine he was prepared to take—not yet.

One Sunday, Søren read the Gospel story of the disciples who, frightened at their teacher's crucifixion, barricaded themselves in an upper room refuge. Søren felt much like them, conflicted and scared, at once relentlessly seeking the divine, studying theology and even reading Scripture, and yet hiding out from the living God. The disciples were taken completely by surprise when Jesus showed up saying, "Peace be with you." If Jesus was going to get to him too, Søren realized, it would only be through firmly locked doors. And yet, unexpectedly, that is just what the resurrected Jesus did. On May 19, 1838, Søren had a decisive spiritual experience, a feeling of "indescribable joy" that was inexplicable to his rational mind. In that mysterious moment, the young man arrived at his life's central truth at last—the realization that, at his core, he was a person found by God.

The young man who had long examined belief from an intellectual distance, standing outside it, now threw himself into an inward, ardent Christianity. (Søren Kierkegaard is not called the father of existentialism for nothing.) Søren well knew that his individual relationship with God was a radical choice. As he put it, faith is an either-or. It is either God or—well, the rest does not matter. Choose what you will, but if you choose anything other than God, you lose out; both you and your choices are lost. Søren embraced faith as a passion, a leap to live life in its fullest sense.

The newly committed Søren wanted to bear witness to Jesus Christ but not, he said, in the way of the "parsons' trash" peddled by his own state church, the self-satisfied institution that counted all Danish citizens as automatic Christians from birth. Thoughtless piety made him want to scream. Søren disdained the complacent neighbors who were no better than baptized pagans, oblivious to sincere, transformative spirituality.

And so, out to provoke the bored religious folks around him, Søren became a kind of literary prankster. He wrote aesthetic, philosophical, and polemical volumes, journal essays and popular newspaper articles. Leafing through his collected works, the philosopher in me wanders along, playing the philosophy game. It doesn't take long to get lost in

Søren's complex writings on subjective truth, objective truth, dread, existence, irony.

Then Søren surprises with a jab. Don't just *be* a Christian, he says, as if "Christian" is some assigned label that you're simply stuck with forever, an identity that means nothing to you. No, take all of your life to *become* a Christian: choose, again and again with each new day, to be a real self, an authentic person in relation to God. Abandon your calculated safety for a reckless, wholehearted life of faith in Christ. Continue to become. Grow. Risk. Take that radical leap of faith, right now.

Sometimes I presume my faith, as if I were a smug Danish Christian, detached and drifting in and out of convinced belief in God. My spirit floats somewhere beyond the embodied decisions I make in everyday life. The vital energy that wakes me up in the morning is spent on temporary tasks and immediate concerns, heedless of the demanding Jesus who waits at the locked door of my heart. My deeper impulses doze, sometimes undetectable.

How will my soul wake up to the risky joy of authentic faith? It is anguished, struggling Søren who shows me the path into unreserved living—mind, body, and soul, fully aware. I find that once Søren experienced the faith that reached beyond abstract knowledge, it was the practice of prayer that kindled his inner transformation. "The function of prayer is not to influence God," he said, "but rather to change the nature of the one who prays." Growing into a fervent person of prayer with living faith as his aim, Søren's daily encounters with the eternal became as essential to him as breathing.

It's no surprise that we don't all know the devotional side of Søren. Renowned as a celebrity poet, critic, agitator, and philosopher, he was reserved about his own private devotional life. Even as he was perfectly comfortable ranting against the Danish church or dashing off clever magazine editorials, he confessed that baring the intimacies of his life with God was "so difficult, so difficult."

I wonder if Søren felt like I sometimes do—that while my public Christian self can lead Bible studies and discuss theology, I am oddly hesitant, at the same time, to speak about my raw, honest connection with God. That might seem strange to the many forthright people who open their faithful hearts to anyone who will listen. I resonate with Søren as he reflects on his personal spiritual life: "My inwardness is too true for me to be able to talk about it."

Prayer, Søren's ongoing conversation with God, becomes the source of his greatest earthly happiness. Søren likens prayer to a gyroscope, a practice that balances him come what may. Happily for you and me, he recorded his prayers in a journal. On those pages Søren speaks frankly to God of his questions, confidence, doubts, joys, pains, consolation, suffering, love, longing, depression. It's all there. And finally he arrives at gratitude. "It is wonderful how God's love overwhelms me," he writes. There is no truer prayer than the one Søren utters over and over: the prayer of thanks to God for doing so indescribably much more than he'd ever expected.

This morning, as autumn begins, I'm swept up into the urgent. Big thoughts of purpose are pushed aside. Quiet, leisurely devotion would be a luxury. As restless Søren kept moving, I will also dash through many miles today. But before I do, Søren's wise words come to me, "The best help in all action is to pray; that is true genius. Then one never goes wrong." Leave it to an existentialist philosopher to pull me back into the present moment.

No longer a caricature of the brooding, angst-ridden intellectual, Søren prompts me to take down the coffee-stained volume of one hundred prayers and approach God in his company. *Father in Heaven!* we begin. *Help us never forget that You are love. This conviction will triumph in our hearts, even if the coming day brings inquietude, anxiety, fright or distress.* Soul brother Søren, so traumatized by his father's fearful fundamentalist religion, was once found by a great divine love. Now he urges me to take the risk and go deeper, to fling myself into God's presence—and know the one good, unshakeable thing in life.

Reconsider Sainthood

You, O Lord, never ceased to watch over my secret heart.

The only "saints" honored in my family's Protestant home were stern, unadorned men explicitly named in the New Testament—Saint Paul and Saint Peter, for starters. I, on the other hand, was reliably convicted and named a depraved sinner in every Sunday sermon, even before I had finished third grade! Sure, biblical saints were admirable—but when you got right down to it, who would want be around one of those guys? Preferring a little pizzazz, I envisioned more contemplative saints on a high holy plane, floating on clouds of mystical bliss. Audacious saints leaping into the trenches of evil, wrangling demons into submission. Imperturbable saints serenely proclaiming their faith while being mauled by voracious coliseum lions. But still: not likely to feature in my future.

Back then, I figured that it was easy enough to tell saints from sinners; if I'd walked the college neighborhood where I live now, I would have declared it Sin Central, though Rugby Road is no different from many campuses after a Friday night. Shattered liquor bottles and crushed beer cans litter the sidewalk. Empty kegs and sodden couches on fraternity house lawns testify to the university's number one party school ranking, chosen by *Playboy* on the basis of three categories: sex, nightlife, and sports.

If *Playboy* had thrown ancient Roman schools into its competition, the University of Carthage would have been in the running for the title. In the sex category, UCarthage boasted the goddess Coelestis, a pagan "Queen of Heaven" celebrated with popular displays of live fornication. Sports? Chariot contests at the racetrack brought out screaming crowds. Nightlife featured fortune tellers, communal baths, and X-rated theater productions. From then till now, from North Africa to North America, college kids do love to party.

❧ ❧ ❧

A certain UCarthage freshman named Augustine was no exception. He arrived from his backwater Algerian hometown of Thagaste ready to revel. "I came to Carthage," Augustine recalls, "where all around me hissed a cauldron of illicit loves." A "muddy carnal concupiscence" filled the air as the bubbling impulses of late adolescence befogged and obscured the young man's heart. Augustine already had a record of drinking, stealing, and promiscuity. He ran with a group of wild proto-fraternity brothers called the Wreckers. By age eighteen, he'd fathered a baby with his girlfriend, a young woman considered below his social standing. Looking back on his college days, Augustine ranked himself among the worst sinners ever.

I'm not perfect; that's obvious to anyone who's been with me for about three minutes. So long as someone draws a bright line dividing sinner and saint, I'll end up on the lively sinner's side, though minus the hissing cauldron, thanks. Still, I'm beginning to feel like there's something off about the way we keep our distance from the "saints," those Special Ones who've been officially beatified and certified by distant church officials, held up as perfection incarnate. The real-life bio of the great "Saint" Augustine turns the old pious distinctions upside down. It may be better to reconsider definitions after all. Perhaps try something like: a saint is a sinner too—but is someone who, by God's grace, goes through life in the spirit of Christ.

Consider Augustine as a rowdy teenager—you'd never have pegged him as saint material. He was a person with a story, a story of sinning and seeking, a story of divine surprises. For this I love Augustine; he gives us all hope that God may make something terrific of us yet. Even young Augustine's own mother, Monica, had serious doubts about the state of his soul. She fretted over her boy, and for good reason.

Devout Monica was like other helicopter moms through the ages. She'd raised her son in the church and urged him to follow Christ, but he would have none of it. In desperation, she turned to a local pastor and begged him to persuade her wayward son to take up the Christian faith. The minister declined, wise enough to know that force was pointless. "Let him be where he is," he assured her, "only pray the Lord for him. It cannot be that the son of these tears should perish." And so Monica prayed for her wayward son. And prayed and prayed and prayed.

Meanwhile, life at the university promised social advancement, intellectual reward, and physical pleasure. Augustine was captivated by the cutting-edge philosophy trending with his classmates. Compared to the unsophisticated scriptures of his hometown Christian religion, the teachings of the great Roman orator Cicero seemed eloquent and wise.

Once he finished at the top of his rhetoric class, ambitious Augustine took his Carthaginian girlfriend and young son across the sea to Rome, where he landed a teaching position in Milan. When mother Monica, who'd managed to get herself across the Mediterranean, deemed the partner and child to be a drag on her son's career, the two were shipped back to North Africa. Monica found a more suitable fiancée (both Christian *and* rich) and made the match, but since the bride-to-be was still too young to marry, the wedding was on hold. In the meantime, our forlorn professor found that he just couldn't get by without sexual intimacy; he found a lover.

Augustine was attracted to the ideal of the cultivated, tranquil life, inspired by Cicero's words: "By the guidance of wisdom, one may become a good and a happy man," and "Prudence, reason and reflection ought to rule all other powers of the mind." Yet Augustine's personal spiritual reality was a confusion of loneliness, addiction, and guilt. Amidst his professional success, Augustine asked himself, *"Of what profit to me was my nimble wit in those sciences and all those knotty volumes" if my conscience is unrelieved?*

Then Augustine met an unexpected Christian, a generous man he saw to be honored by people of importance, a lucky man by worldly standards whose intelligence rivaled his own. The man was Ambrose, the dynamic bishop of Milan, whose smart sermons intrigued Augustine. Ambrose's teaching built a bridge between the philosophical wisdom of Cicero and the deeper truth of Christ. I find it beautiful of God to attract skeptical Augustine through a caring new friend who was worthy of his gifted mind and accepting of his struggling heart.

Augustine's memoir, *Confessions*, recounts a growing tension: beyond the intellectual wrangling, a spiritual crisis emerged. Would he decide for God or against God? Augustine writes that time and again he was on the edge, believing, ready to die to death and come alive to life. Augustine hesitated, for he knew that if he decided for God, it would mean abandoning his old pleasure-seeking compulsions.

Conflicted, he prayed, "God, grant me chastity and continence," then added, "but not yet!" Sometimes he'd beg for liberation, crying, "Let it be now, let it be now!" even as he played for more time, held back by his bad habits, those sketchy companions who just wouldn't release their grip on him. He lamented, "I felt that I was still the captive of my sins, and in misery I kept crying, 'How long shall I go on saying, Tomorrow, tomorrow? Why not now? Why not make an end of my ugly sins at this moment?'" Ready to give up, he flung himself down on the ground in frustrated tears.

It's a famous scene in the annals of Christian conversion stories. Augustine was lying under a fig tree in full tantrum mode, sobbing so loudly that he nearly missed a small, high voice singing through the garden. Was it a boy? Was it a girl? He couldn't say. But the child was chanting the refrain, "Take it and read, take it and read." Augustine looked up, puzzled. *Take it and read?* What kind of childhood game was this? He'd certainly never played it before.

What a strange way to hear from God. The Holy One didn't arrive in a consuming fire or a supernatural lightning bolt. No intellectually compelling sermon prompted a tearful walk down the aisle at the altar call. Instead, God invited Augustine into a game, calling out as a sweetly melodic child, a chant heard across the orchard.

Augustine realized in a flash that *Take it and read* was a prompt to open the Scripture. As he grabbed a Bible, the book fell open to Romans 13, the passage that reads, "Not in reveling and drunkenness, not in lust and wantonness, not in quarrels and rivalries. Rather, arm yourself with the Lord Jesus Christ; spend no more thought on nature and nature's appetites." Wow. Verses on the mark, just for him.

As he read Paul's words, Augustine felt confidence flood his heart and light dispel his dark doubts. The Holy Spirit released Augustine from himself, loosening the tangles that had tied him up inside. The young man marked the place and closed the book.

How did this radical, redemptive moment come about after such long struggle? In the end, Augustine exhausted his own strength, his own intelligence, his own ambition. He had not been rescued by his attempts to change himself. Not even his belief in God was enough. Liberation came from without: not through a sophisticated philosophical argument but in a simple, playful, divine invitation.

And so it was, dear reader, that Augustine the sinner became a saint, as well.

That ambitious reveler at the University of Carthage went on to be a role model of faith, even for us Protestants. The journey to get there was rough; Augustine suffered through broken relationships, destructive habits, intellectual crises, and emotional ups and downs. But at long last God intervened and freed Augustine out of his divided self.

Augustine's journey took him right back where he started: Africa. After his spiritual surrender, Augustine returned to form a Christian community. For many years he served as a priest and then as a bishop, writing, preaching, and serving the church even as invading Vandals battered at the gates of the city and the Roman Empire fell.

❧ ❧ ❧

I used to assume that the spiritual life would be a straightforward matter. That I'd have power over my circumstances and over my feelings. That I could change course anytime, if only I followed the script I learned in Sunday school, a simple narrative that goes like this: (1) repent of your sins, (2) invite Jesus into your heart, and (3) prepare to enjoy your new life of happy blessing. Augustine's story, ancient as it is, feels familiar to me now. My own experiences have shown me how wrenching it can be to come to God, even when I want it, caught as I am between false freedoms and vulnerable faith.

Practiced patterns linger. I read an inspiring article, listen to a Ted Talk, or hear a rousing sermon and get a glimpse of the person I want to be. I make my resolutions (Commit to the Body Pump class. Start the day in prayer. Pass on the pinot noir. Say three kind things to my spouse each day), but twenty-four hours into every fresh start, I'm screwing up. My vices may seem minor compared to those you'll find on Rugby Road, but temptations still trip me. I am in excellent company with Augustine, the sinner saint.

Augustine's one-liner is a classic: "God, You have formed us for Yourself, and our hearts are restless till they find rest in You." Yes, I often feel restless, far from God and even lost to myself. Apparently blind alleys and bypasses are part of the pilgrimage. Moments of joy and revelations of grace follow frustrated hopes and inward pains. I stumble along, taking the long route to peace. Down the road, older and wiser, I may recall Augustine's prayer, "You, O Lord, never ceased to watch over my secret heart," and ask myself: Was this the way to sainthood all along?

Thérèse of Lisieux 1873–1897

Take the Little Way

Jesus does not demand great deeds.

All He wants is self-surrender and gratitude.

A GRACIOUS HOME TO WELCOME THE world, an experiment in community, an expression of lived faith, and an invitation to thoughtful exchange. We envisioned all this (and more) when Charles and I and our three kids fastened the bronze plaque onto the freshly painted front door, announcing: Bonhoeffer House.

The child of a minister and oldest of five children, I grew up in a household where our shoes were lined up on Saturday nights, newly polished for church the next morning. Sundays brought extra guests to the dinner table; my unflappable mother simply doubled the recipe for macaroni and cheese and mixed up more Lipton instant iced tea. Staying over? She pulled out the sleeper sofa, grabbed a set of sheets from the linen closet. Mom made it look effortless. I believed that I could too. The Bonhoeffer House was ready for visitors and I was up for the venture.

In the seventeen years since we pushed open the Bonhoeffer House doors, the glow is off the golden dream. Cracked radiators, charred lasagna, midnight visitations, roaring undergrad parties next door, cranky kids, sacrificed privacy, and overbooked schedules have chastened our utopian ambitions. The Professor demands quiet; he's got a lecture to write for tomorrow's class. Students are arriving for a Bible study and now Nan urgently requires a ride to volleyball practice. The dinner dishes are congealing on the counter, the dog has raided the trash. I try to keep it together, but beware if you hear me begin to speak in what Nan calls "Mom's real scary quiet voice." I'm about to lose it.

I still long to be that person who loves patiently, believes deeply, lives fully. When I'm frazzled by daily life here, I occasionally entertain that odd, alternative ideal—the one in which I've escaped to a convent, far from this relentless, changeable activity. I imagine myself mindfully present to each moment, centered by peaceful prayer and invigorated by physical labors. When the sisters and I gather in the chapel or weed in the garden, we always know what comes next in the rhythm of community living. With a stripped-down agenda, limited wardrobe options, and a decluttered closet, my mind is clear.

Thérèse of Lisieux shatters my monastic reverie. She left her own comfortable bourgeois home in northwestern France for the convent—and she ended up in an unheated cell, dying of tuberculosis on a straw pallet. Dead at only twenty-four, she'd accomplished so little that the other nuns had nothing to write about in her obituary. I'll bet that Thérèse had her own romantic visions of shared life; she must have been sorely disappointed.

There are some glaring problems with my own getaway scenario too. My husband is missing from the picture, and I couldn't do without Henry, Will, Nan, or our dog Ginger. The flowing nun's habit? Most definitely *not* my look. Total obedience to superiors? Never. I know I'm just daydreaming a way to be stronger and more spiritual, calmer and more focused.

The story of Thérèse, aka "The Little Flower," is a backwards fairy tale, from silk slippers to rough sandals. Like me, our heroine was one of five children born into a respectable Christian family. Her super devout parents kept up a regimen of daily prayer (at 5:30 a.m.!), regular fasting and Sabbath observance. Thérèse loved God from day one, claiming that even as a toddler she'd never refused God anything.

Thérèse's first few years were golden. Her four older sisters pampered her, her parents found her adorable. Everything on earth smiled at her; she found blossoms under her feet. Then, when Thérèse was only four, her mother, Zélie, died. Her sisters all left to become nuns. Without her family to shelter her, Thérèse was sickened by grief.

But Thérèse had boldness at her core. The valiant little girl decided to devote her whole life to God. Planning her future, she fantasized that she'd grow up to be a soldier, an apostle, a hermit, a missionary, or even a priest. No surprise: none of these careers were open to nineteenth-century village maidens. And so, at nine years old, Thérèse marched, with utter confidence, to enlist at the local Carmelite monastery. The nuns sent her back to her father. She was, of course, too young.

Thérèse waited impatiently and then returned to the convent gate at age fourteen, ready to begin her awesome new career. But she was refused again. When she met Pope Leo VIII during a family pilgrimage to Rome, the desperate girl saw her chance. She got right up in the pope's face and begged him to pull some strings. The flustered pope muttered something about obeying her superiors. Thérèse turned up the volume, clutching his legs, refusing to budge. As the papal guards dragged the sobbing girl toward the door, Pope Leo passed the problem off to God, saying, "Go . . . Go . . . you will enter if God wills it."

Back home in Lisieux, she was promptly admitted to the convent. (I ask you: Was it divine providence or stubborn melodrama that unlocked the door?) She had arrived at last. To the Carmelite convent, where all was silence except for the sweep of long habits and the hiss of rope sandals along the echoing hallways. Here was a physical grace and order she craved. She was delivered from her stifling, overstuffed middle-class childhood and into her life's calling: to adore Jesus utterly.

Thérèse's vivid spiritual imagination comes through in her memoir. In many ways, it's like any teenaged girl's diary. The pages burst with capital letters, exclamation points and images of pretty flowers, victims, salty tears, little angels, martyrs, consuming fire. One biographer said that reading the book feels like eating too many marshmallows. But Thérèse isn't writing about flirtations with cute boys; she's all about abandonment to her beloved Jesus. Thérèse writes of scaling the summit of the mountain of love to demonstrate her total trust in God. She describes Jesus leading her into a "furnace of divine love."

As she writes, Thérèse imagines herself into the story of Jesus by the well. When he asks for water, she's the humble Samaritan woman with a cup in her hand, saying, "I am only a very little soul, who can offer very little things to our Lord." Thérèse often speaks of taking the Little Way, where every small action, every unseen sacrifice—even a drink of water—is a full surrender to the tenderness of Jesus' infinite love.

"My God, I choose all! I do not wish to be a saint by halves," she prays. Ever the go-getter, Thérèse envisions bold saints out there, doing big things for God in the world. She admires an earlier French girl, Joan of Arc, valiant in bloody combat for the Lord of Hosts. But little Thérèse? Though she burns to do battle for God's glory, her war will never be on the open field; instead, she is a prisoner of Love, forever cut off from the world, held captive within the cloister. Choosing the Little Way will be Thérèse's ultimate challenge. The great demand to submit her will to God in everything.

Let us keep far from all that glitters, she would say, and learn to love our littleness. Follow this Little Way with an attitude of lowliness, poorness of spirit, trust. Let us even be satisfied to feel nothing as we serve God and others whenever and wherever we can. It is then, however obscure and unnoticed we may be, that Jesus will come to seek us out and transform us with his love.

Yes, Thérèse was given to austere heroics and interior struggles. By her telling, suffering intensifies devotion. After all the years of planning, praying, and envisioning her ecstatic life with God, she must have been privately disenchanted by how things turned out. I imagine the teenaged Thérèse, realizing that she's truly stuck for life inside an obscure convent in chilly Lisieux. She's crowded in with much older nuns who apparently do not share her passion for Christlike loving service. In fact, the sisters annoy her in a million little ways.

Here's a snapshot. Each day, Thérèse patiently escorts a sick, irritable sister from prayers to dinner, cuts her bread, endures her criticisms. Thérèse's humanity comes through at prayer, as the young woman fights to concentrate while another sister rattles her rosary beads incessantly. She writes, "Perhaps none heard it but myself, for my hearing is extremely acute, and I cannot say how it tormented me!" At work, washing handkerchiefs in the laundry, the nun seated close by constantly "besprinkles" Thérèse with filthy water (on purpose?). Though Thérèse is tempted to make a show of wiping off her face, she bears the offenses uncomplainingly. Still, I'll bet that some nights she lay on her pallet wondering why God had ever inspired her with such fantastical, unfulfilled dreams.

Thérèse was a tough girl who stayed in there. She didn't hide behind abstractions or doctrine; she was about action. She put it simply, saying, "Jesus does not demand great deeds. All He wants is self-surrender and gratitude. That is all Jesus asks from us. He needs nothing from us except our love." Day in and day out, Thérèse lived an ordinary witness of extraordinary love—theology on its knees. Though the Little Way brought her no glory, she chose it anyway.

Whenever the nuns got on her saintly nerves, Thérèse made a choice: to treat them as companions whom she dearly loved. To get there, Thérèse adopted the "fake till you make it" approach. "When I suffer much, when things that are painful and disagreeable befall me," she said, "instead of assuming an air of sadness, I respond by a smile." Reading her words, I feel my teeth clench at the forced cheer.

Still, I'll give the young woman credit. She always did defy expectations, even at the end when she was dying of tuberculosis at twenty-four. Where Kierkegaard made a leap of faith, his intellectual vault over the abyss of doubt into Christian faith, Thérèse took the Little Way, a brave emotional vault over the abyss of self-interest and into radical Christian love.

❧ ❧ ❧

I've always seen the youthful Thérèse and the teenaged Karen as different girls—Thérèse scribbling quaint piety and Karen analyzing a Vonnegut novel. Thérèse repeating Latin prayers and Karen cramming for the A.P. biology exam. Recently I dug out my old high school diary and, faced with my own handwriting, I felt a peculiar sensation. There were no capital letters (my e e cummings phase) among the words: "i will act and trust that god has honored my feeble desire to praise him through my life." I found a prayer in which I wrote, "i believe that what i do makes a difference. my time is valuable. but you are god. my little efforts are worthless until you bless them and fill them with your power. here am i. send me." I heard the voice of a fervently believing Karen, the idealistic adolescent I once was.

I still have lofty notions, but the convent-as-spiritual-spa-getaway won't be happening. Thérèse quickly discovered that the cloister would not be all tranquility, glowing beeswax candles and choral polyphony. It was a place of affliction. The Carmelite sisters endured restricted sleep, no travel, no comforts, no easy conversation, no family or romantic attachments. No freedom. Daily religious life would sorely try Thérèse's single vocation, her sole occupation: *to love*.

In the grind, it was no easy thing to abandon herself utterly, unflinchingly to God. Still, she chose to take the Little Way, no matter how difficult. As usual, she made up her mind, saying, "Out of love I will suffer and, out of love, rejoice." When she folded the laundry, scrubbed the cold stone floors or knelt before the altar, she would do it all for love. "In everything I must find self-denial and sacrifice," she pledged.

Ah, the martyr complex. We've all seen it, the person who sighs theatrically and says, "Don't mind me! You go first/make the decision/have the last piece of cake/let me wash all the pots. It's fine, *really*." I may tend to play the victim myself, though I won't admit to it here. (I truly prefer burned toast.) But Thérèse takes self-denial to an extreme. Her high-pitched virtue grates on me; all the suffering talk makes me queasy.

And now? I'd truly be acting the martyr if I claimed that life in the Bonhoeffer House is rough. I have privilege and comfort beyond compare. Honestly, though, the experience of sharing my family, privacy and possessions is not the unmitigated joy that Charles and I once thought it would be. Real experiences rarely are. I didn't see what was coming when I prayed, "here i am. send me."

Life goes on. I am no Little Flower. I am often ambitious and restless. Thérèse and I still deeply disagree over the merits of self-denial, but I've come to respect that bold child who banged on the doors of the convent as a nine-year-old, marched up to the pope in Rome, and mastered the grueling monastic routines, all for the love of Christ. When dreams of the Christian life disappoint, I recall the Little Way of Thérèse. What might it mean to learn to love my littleness? To serve without demanding praise—or even satisfaction? Here and now, with all that I know, I consider the confines of this place and this day. The invitation into my own Little Way.

C. S. LEWIS 1898–1963

Wake Up to Joy

It was a sensation, of course, of desire . . .
an unsatisfied desire which is more desirable
than any other satisfaction. I call it Joy.

DAVID WAS A PHILOSOPHY MAJOR, a regular guest at the Bonhoeffer House during his college years who sat politely through weekly lunch conversations about Christian faith. Afterward, I'd often get emails from him, ones that began with an apology like, "I didn't want to ask this question in front of the whole the group. I hope you won't be shocked," and led into tough questions about God. "How can I believe in a God who allows little children to be tortured and die?" Tough, intelligent questions. Personal, searching questions. "Why did my best high school friend suffer depression and die by suicide? Why couldn't I save him?" David took a clear-eyed look at the real world around him and had to ask: "Is Christianity a cruel myth?"

David didn't need to worry about offending me. I'm not one to be exasperated by challenges to Christian faith; they come to me unbidden. So many mornings the *New York Times* delivers another installment of misery, and a voice inside my head asks if God is real. Faced with the photograph of a distraught mother cradling her murdered toddler, my stomach tightens. It does no good to rationalize.

❧ ❧ ❧

Atheism has its champions today; check out the nonfiction bestseller list for the current favorites. When Richard Dawkins, the Oxford evolutionary biologist and skeptic, came to speak at the university, I was among the standing-room-only crowd in Old Cabell Hall. I'd skimmed his book *The God Delusion*, so I wasn't surprised when Dawkins ripped the viability of belief. In his persuasive English accent, Dawkins declared that the scientific view of the world is wholly incompatible with religion; faith is downright toxic, a betrayal of sound thinking, a rejection of all that's best about our humanity. Believers are gullible and superstition is dangerous, so let's all get over it.

But before Dawkins, another brainy Brit named C. S. "Jack" Lewis also dismissed religion as irrational folly. Jack was only nine when his beloved mother, Flora, died an agonizing death to cancer. Young Jack never really got along with Albert, the father who packed him off to a dreary boarding school where the schoolmaster was declared insane. The lonely, heartbroken boy repudiated the duty-bound Christian faith of his family, the dull tradition that gave him no comfort at all. Defying orthodoxy, he braced himself with a materialistic view of the world and turned to rational hard science to explain everything.

When asked about his religious views, seventeen-year-old Jack declared, "I believe in no religion. There is absolutely no proof for any of them, and from a philosophical standpoint Christianity is not even the best." If that boy had stood with me in Old Cabell Hall, he would have cheered when Richard Dawkins said, "Faith is the great cop-out, the great excuse to evade the need to think and evaluate evidence."

An extremely bright young man, Jack was admitted to Oxford University in 1917. World War I disrupted his academic haven before he'd even settled in. He joined the British army and spent his nineteenth birthday in France's Somme Valley, sickened by scenes of horribly wounded men and smashed corpses. Nonetheless, back in Oxford after what they called the Great War, the twenty-one-year-old wounded veteran bragged that he had never once called upon any desperately imagined God, not even under attack in the foxhole.

Jack lived by scholarly logic and intelligence and the wish to keep his soul unfettered. Yet in spite of himself, Jack's imagination drew him to myth and story. In an ineffable flashback, he was transported to an early morning at the Old House when his brother Warnie brought a little terrarium into the nursery. Within the childhood memory, Jack was overwhelmed by a feeling: a sensation of desire. Before Jack could capture a glimpse of that which he desired, the powerful feeling was gone. The world had turned commonplace again. Jack was captivated by this longing, the unsatisfied desire that is itself more desirable than any other pleasure. He named the feeling Joy.

What is the source of this fleeting Joy? For years, Jack would hold the question. As a fellow and tutor at Oxford, he tried on atheism, materialism, idealism. "I'm not the religious type," Jack wrote. "I want to be let alone, to feel I'm my own." But no glib and shallow rationalism could account for the mysterious richness of real things. Even his literary, philosophical readings kept bringing him back to Christianity.

Frankly, Jack dreaded the steady, unrelenting approach of the very one whom he had so earnestly desired not to meet: God. After years of wrangling and resisting, Jack felt that he was out of options. One night, alone in his university room, he gave in, admitted that God was God, and knelt and prayed: the most dejected and "reluctant convert in all England."

What was it that compelled the stubborn, scholarly Jack Lewis toward faith in Christ? It was the old ache that whispered within him from early childhood: Joy, that powerful, painful feeling of longing, that key to transcendence, which opened up an existence beneath and beyond this one. In his logical way, Jack considered his own desire, the experience that nothing in this world could satisfy, and concluded that he was made for another world. Beyond the scope of human reason, Jack reckoned, there must be far more than meets the calculating eye.

In the end, God, the true source of Joy, captivated Jack's restless mind and seeking heart. Jack returned, at age thirty-one, to his cradle faith—but this time he embraced the Christian story not through fear or duty but out of a brave willingness to be charmed by a big, beautiful story.

God was the object of Jack's lifelong quest; the revelation was profound. Christianity made reasonable sense of things at last, far more sense than his earlier atheism ever had. Jack came to believe Christianity just as he believed that the sun rises: not only could he see the sun, but by it he could see everything else. In the light of imaginative faith, Jack could discern the intrinsic interconnectedness of things. Through the eyes of faith, the world was reenchanted.

❧ ❧ ❧

The astronomer Carl Sagan concluded that the cosmos contains all that is or ever will be. Coming from a contemporary scientist, that's no surprise. Even if I could have persuaded Carl Sagan to read Jack's *Mere Christianity* and then buy into Jack's philosophical arguments for Christianity, he'd still have more than enough existential, ethical justifications for rejecting religious conviction. Look: the world is filled with both beauty and horror. People inflict terrible cruelty on one another. Close to home, there's Holly's divorce. Tom's crushed hopes. Rob's stroke. Sara's early death. There's just no way to keep the shine on a cheerful Christian faith in the face of inexhaustible suffering. Can any honest faith take hard things into account?

Even Jack, who'd become renowned as the great champion of Christianity, was felled by grief when Joy Davidman, the surprise late love of his life, died of cancer despite his anguished prayers. Jack was forced to reconsider the deity in whom he'd come to believe, tempted toward terrible conclusions about God. Had he been all wrong about Joy, desire, the promise of a glorious heaven?

In the face of dilemmas like these, atheists like Richard Dawkins admit no divine meaning, no ultimate purpose in the universe—and they certainly perceive no goodness there. Sure, they say, we cope with life's struggles by inventing ideas of goodness and morality, but it's all just pathetic make-believe based on nothing. Like many thinking people, they look out and see a flat, godless terrain; they have their reasons to dismiss Christianity.

And yet. Carl Sagan hints at something more, in words that sound eerily like Jack's. The scientist writes, "Our feeblest contemplations of the Cosmos stir us—there is a tingling in the spine, a catch in the voice, a faint sensation, as if a distant memory, of falling from a height. We know we are approaching the greatest of mysteries."

And yet. The greatest of mysteries stirs us. In his time of grief, Jack had a fresh experience of imagination. He dreamed that he was trapped in an airless, lightless dungeon, despairing and alone. But then he heard a faint sound from far off. Was it the echo of waves or wind-blown trees, perhaps some cattle lowing? In that moment Jack realized that he was not locked in a cellar after all, but free, out in the entirely black but open night air. Then he heard another sound, a smaller sound, just close at hand—a chuckle of laughter; a friend was beside him in the shadow. It was, Jack thought, "a good, good sound." The world, which had seemed bleakly tragic, was gently restored with hope and a flash of the old Joy.

When I find myself in the dark, I return to Jack's beloved stories, The Chronicles of Narnia. There I find Lucy Pevensie, the girl exiled by war to a strange place, hiding in the back of a deep wardrobe. Unable to see, Lucy fumbles among the mothballed coats only to step through into Narnia, a forest of fresh snowfall, glistening and cold. On her adventures with her sister and brothers through the magical new land of fawns, witches, and talking animals, Lucy encounters Aslan, the majestic lion. "Dearest daughter," Aslan says, "I knew you would not be long in coming to me. Joy shall be yours." Lucy the lost is found.

Like Lucy, I fumble and hide. Yet I, too, experience the unplanned, uncontrolled incursions of God into my life. On the most ordinary of days there are the good, good sounds of my daughter, Nan, as she sings beyond her bedroom door. Of Henry's unexpected voice booming through the phone. Of Charles muttering a line of poetry to himself. Of Will's band, Gold Connections, rocking out over the radio. The good, good sounds of the people I love. Illuminations of Joy. I find that I am in the free, open air after all.

Jack points me toward what is most true—and it's a truth strong enough to reenchant my very life. My skeptical friend David and I still engage in our philosophical debates, though along the way we've realized that we can't intellectualize our way into honest faith. That is more a work of heart and soul. Yet David has come to believe in the deeper magic too: the ultimate triumph of life over death, the more real reality of heaven. When we speak of God now, we take care and wait with hope. At any moment Joy—the intimation of eternity and antiquity and enormity—may arrive.

Henri Nouwen 1932–1996

Be the Beloved

The truth, even though I cannot feel it right now,
is that I am the chosen child of God, precious in God's eyes,
called the Beloved from all eternity, and held safe.

No doubt about it: Thomas Jefferson was the kind of energetic, capable leader Americans love. I clamber through the brilliant late-autumn forest as if by command of the master of the mountain, hiking up what's been called the "steep, savage hill." At the summit, the shaded path opens onto a wide lawn and there, above the clouds, stands his neoclassical mansion, Monticello. As a man, Jefferson is an icon of upward mobility: the intelligent and ambitious patriot who transformed the young country and established the University of Virginia.

But given my choice of public intellectuals, I'll take Henri J. M. Nouwen over Thomas Jefferson any day. As a well-loved religion professor at Harvard and Yale, Henri packed out the university halls. On one occasion, so many people sat on the floor and crowded into the hallway that Henri promised an encore lecture to anyone who would give up their seat. The volunteers who left and returned the following night found the auditorium filled to capacity all over again. Clearly, this Henri guy was no ordinary Ivy League highbrow.

The first time I read Henri, I felt the difference for myself. The subtitle of his book prompted me to pick it up: *A Journey Through Anguish to Freedom*. There for all to read was the revered teacher's secret journal, a raw account of his depression, his questions, his disappointments. I could hardly believe how bravely Henri laid bare his life. Though the pain nearly destroyed him, Henri wrote later, all of his agony would become "like fertile ground for greater trust, stronger hope, and deeper love." I could learn something from this scholar.

❧ ❧ ❧

As a little boy, Henri survived the trauma of Holland's Nazi occupation. Wartime privation and chronic anxiety left him with a spiritual craving too: a hunger for Jesus. He channeled his deep restiveness to pursue the priesthood, graduate studies in modern psychology, and an academic career. Even as he advanced through the ranks of elite academic institutions, Henri was never content to just *talk* about God. He warned that words, lectures, books, and programs about the spiritual life get in the way of the Spirit itself. Henri brought both his soul and his intellect into the classroom, longing to communicate the living presence of Christ to his students.

As erudite as he was, Henri wrote his many books in a simple, pastoral style. He is open about his struggles to answer the lifelong question, "Who am I?" Henri gets me. He knows that I am seduced by the inner voice of ambition that says, "I am what I accomplish," "I am what others think of me," and "I am what I have." So long as my sense of self-identity depends on external things, my mental energy is spent just staying above the line, on keeping it together. I'm at the mercy of others who tell me how I'm doing, but this is not a safe place to be.

Jefferson was the poster child for overachievers: architect, philosopher, scholar, lawyer, author of the Declaration of Independence, and, oh yeah, president. He bragged that over the course of fifty years the sun had never caught him in bed; he rose as soon as he could see the hands of the mantel clock mounted at the foot of his bed. After all, he's the man who said, "Determine never to be idle. It is wonderful how much may be done if we are always doing." I'd wager that Jefferson's "pursuit of happiness" was not for slackers.

Henri was a doer too. He was adored by readers all over the world and revered by his students. He published a book every year and was in constant demand to lecture, counsel, travel, pastor, and visit friends. Henri received quite a bit of affirmation. Yet there was another side to him—an anxious man with a "habitual, almost neurotic need to be needed." Private contention over his homosexuality and the loneliness of a celibate vow troubled him deeply.

Throughout his life, Henri was caught up in a cycle of long, hectic days of teaching and service, followed by periods of nervous exhaustion, depression, and insomnia. He knew what it meant to wonder, "If the people who so admire me could know me in my innermost self, would they still love me?" Henri's pursuit of significance nearly killed him.

Into our universal struggle for success, love and security, Henri inserts one central, countercultural Christian declaration: "At the core of my faith belongs the conviction that we are the beloved sons and daughters of God." He takes this startling truth from Jesus, that same Jesus who heard God's words spoken over him at his Jordan River baptism: *You are my beloved Child and my favor rests on you.*

Henri endeavered to follow his own advice: stay home and pray. Settle in to your own belovedness. The central spiritual task, for Henri and you and me, is to grasp the truth of our belovedness and then live a life grounded in that deep realization. "That's not very easy," Henri admits. "In fact, most of us fail constantly to claim the truth of who we are." I agree with Henri on this one. I'm distracted by the painful awareness of my faults, my weaknesses, my inadequacies; all the things I'm not. I've heard about God's unconditional love for me but still I contradict the sacred voice that calls me by name: the beloved.

Henri changed his life. He chose to follow a radically different path: the way of downward mobility. The brilliant professor left Harvard at the peak of his academic career. He walked away from professional security and moved to L'Arche ("the Ark"), an organization founded by the Catholic philosopher Jean Vanier. At L'Arche, people living with intellectual disabilities and those who come to help them share daily life together as equal members. Now a worldwide network of residential communities, L'Arche was established on the principle that each and every person brings a unique, mysterious value to the group. At L'Arche, those who are viewed as defective or worthless by the outside world are just as precious as those who have accomplished material success.

Newly arrived, Henri took on the job of direct-care assistant to Adam Arnett, a young member who could not move by himself or even speak. Scholarly credentials surely meant nothing to Adam, who would never read a word of Nouwen's books. Henri had stepped into a wholly different world. Far from the prestigious university, with its academic intensity and cerebral rivalry, L'Arche was a place of "quiet village living, community celebration, the sharing of human vulnerabilities, and an always new invitation to let Jesus be the center of everything."

Caring for Adam taught Henri to focus on *being* rather than *doing*. He knew at last what it meant to be human, Beloved of God, a realization that brought him the hope of God's healing and peace. Henri wrote, "I am a very weak, broken, fragile, and short-living person—but I rejoice in it. I can stand under the cross of my own suffering—or of God's suffering—but I can stand. I don't have to fall apart. I stand with my head erect. I can do that."

❧ ❧ ❧

I don't plan to make any big life transformations just now, not like Henri did. Come back here in a year and you'll likely find me with my family, still doing my job, hustling to answer email, grab coffee with students, respond to the next thing. Chances are I'll look the same, only a little older.

But in the meantime, what if I could truly live into my belovedness? Could I let go of the *doing* to turn toward the *being*? By God's compelling grace I am learning to listen through the noise of accusation and the undercurrent of disquiet. God tells me over and over: you are the beloved in whom I am well pleased. When I am paying attention, I unclench. I'm not being judged. I've got nothing to prove. I'm doing enough. I have enough. I am enough.

Ambition urges me onward and up the mountain. But Henri invites me to look down. He gently asks me to take a closer look at the source of my own value. Henri asks, "Aren't you, like me, hoping that some person, thing or event will come along to give you that final feeling of inner well-being you desire?" My hold on myself is so very fragile. He knows that. So again and again Henri boldly tells me who I truly am. I really don't have to locate my worth in outward success, by way of a blazing career path, or in another's changeable love. I'm not about any of that. At the core of my existence, I am God's beloved. My life is about discovering that I am already, even now, fully loved in Christ. My belovedness in God is the truest thing about me.

When I'm utterly convinced that I am what I can accomplish or possess, Jesus says, "That is a lie." If I'm paying attention, I may hear Jesus whisper, "Repeat after me: 'I am the beloved. God is well pleased with me. Not because people say I'm great, but because God named me the beloved even before I was born.'" The world may reject me, praise me, laugh at, or even spit on me, but no matter what comes, I am the beloved of God. I can live on. Beloved. Beloved. That's who I am. That's who you are.

Flannery O'Connor 1925–1964

Get Down Under Things

I don't want to be doomed to mediocrity in my feeling for Christ. I want to feel. I want to love. Take me, dear Lord, and set me in the direction I am to go.

My family arrived in Atlanta in August, just before school started. To me, the South seemed a different world. The well-mannered, fashion-forward classmates at my new prep school spoke of debutante societies, quail hunting, second homes on Sea Island. They plied me with Krispy Kreme donuts, seafood gumbo, fried catfish, hush puppies, sweet tea, and other delights, as if I were a foreign exchange student from the Philly suburbs. Desperate to fit in, I felt unsophisticated and underdressed. Uninitiated.

What a relief that my father's pastorate, a Presbyterian church downtown, featured the usual: Sunday school, youth group, mid-week prayer meeting, and Sunday night services. There, my new friends and I were all literate in the same Protestant way, versed in the biblical trajectory of creation, sin, guilt, grace, redemption, forgiveness. Solid doctrines that resolved uneasy mystery and pinpointed my place in the universe. The church felt like home.

Just when I was finding my footing, my A.P. English teacher assigned a text by the Georgia author Flannery O'Connor. I casually asked who *he* was (and I didn't make that mistake twice). I was baffled by the O'Connor stories we read in class, alarmed when somebody got gored or blinded or shot. Freaked out by the self-blinding prophet and dying grandmother. Puzzled by the untamed theology of tent meetings. I really couldn't see what Flannery's Jesus-obsessed extremists could say to me, a straight-up kid raised on the Westminster Catechism, the illustrated youth Bible with leatherette cover, and mellow bonfire camp songs. *Who were these Southerners?*

Flannery O'Connor was born in the port city of Savannah, into a South far different from the 1970s Atlanta of malls and movies. The only daughter of devout Catholic parents, Flannery grew up under live oaks and Spanish moss, across the square from the cathedral where she was immersed in ritual, sacraments, and daily mass, sheltered by Sisters of Mercy—a coherent cosmos of faith. Even when her family moved from Savannah to a Milledgeville, Georgia, dairy farm so isolated that it was reached only "by bus or buzzard," Flannery's life centered around God.

Imaginative young Flannery had no trouble amusing herself. She sewed outfits for her chickens and aspired to be a cartoonist. She gave her mother, Regina, a mule for Mother's Day. To the end of her life she had her quirks. She drank Coca-Cola mixed with coffee. She went to bed at nine and said she was always happy to get there.

After graduating from a nearby women's college, Flannery went off to the renowned Writers' Workshop at the University of Iowa. Although she claimed that she didn't know a short story from an ad in the newspaper, Flannery, wholly given to her writing, quickly became a sensation. It is said that she scared the boys to death with her irony. Asked why she wrote, Flannery replied simply, "Because I'm good at it."

Flannery is more forthright in a private prayer: "I do not mean to be clever although I do mean to be clever on 2nd thought and like to be clever and want to be considered so." Confessing feelings of discouragement, she pleads, "Please help me dear God to be a good writer and get something else accepted."

A fellow writer at the Yaddo artist colony described Flannery: "She was a plain sort of young, unmarried girl, a little bit sickly. She had a small-town Southern accent . . . whiny. She whined. She was amusing. She was so gifted, immensely gifted." Though Flannery hardly looked the part, the fiction editor of *Esquire* put her at the red-hot center of his Literary Establishment chart of 1963.

Then, as Flannery's cultural star was on the rise, she was stricken by lupus, an incurable, debilitating disease that sapped her energy and forced her return to the "very muddy and manuery" farm back in Georgia. Confined there, dependent on her mother's care, she wrote only as her diminishing strength permitted—for two hours every morning. Flannery tended a menagerie of peacocks, ducks, and mail-order swans. She knew how matters stood and described them in a letter, "I have enough energy to write with and as that is all I have any business doing anyhow, I can with one eye squinted take it all as a blessing." What you have to measure out, she noted, you come to observe more closely.

Before her death at thirty-nine, Flannery predicted that nobody would write her biography, since lives spent between the house and the chicken yard do not make exciting copy. Yet her outsized spiritual dramas enacted on a Southern stage—told through short stories, novels, and many letters—ensure her place among the greatest American writers, and at the top of my English syllabus.

One cannot get through a Flannery O'Connor story without encountering the strangeness of God. As she said, the greatest dramas involve the salvation or loss of the soul. Her short story "Revelation" startles with its final vision of a field of living fire. The vast hordes of souls rumbling toward heaven, the battalions of freaks and lunatics shouting and clapping and leaping like frogs, are a queerly beautiful sight. And then the words, "In the woods around her the invisible cricket choruses had struck up, but what she heard were the voices of the souls climbing upward into the starry field and shouting hallelujah." Here is a spiritual reality, glorious and disturbing, which my comfortable Christian categories cannot contain.

Where do I experience the shock of mystery in my everyday life? Flannery lamented that our secular society understands the religious mind less and less, that people who believe vigorously in Christ are wholly odd to most readers. It becomes more and more difficult in America to make belief believable, yet this is what she wanted to do. To create fictional examples of radical faith, Flannery went to the old Southern Bible Belt where such people were once taken for granted.

Flannery wrote from what she called a "typical Southern sense of reality." My husband's parents are from Jackson, Mississippi. Charles's mother is lightning quick to assure you that not a single person she's ever known is remotely like any of Flannery's fictional characters, the folks with missing limbs, mysterious bulges, wooden legs, and faces blue with acne. Heavens, no. Yet there they are on the page: Flannery's wart-hogs from hell, misfits and so-called white trash—the peculiar Southerners who lead us to God.

Charles has always been a Flannery O'Connor fan, and he introduced me to her personal correspondence. Flannery's letters reveal a warm, witty, probing woman—nothing like the stern author I'd imagined from her violent stories. She discusses manuscripts she's rewriting, the books she's reading, a funny encounter with the telephone repairman, a promise to send more peacock feathers, news of Cousin Katie, complaints about the "idiot legislature," and an account of a funeral. Throughout the 596 pages, there is a great deal of theology. Flannery insists that she is not a mystic and does not lead a holy life, yet she unapologetically displays her faith: a life of continually turning away from egocentricity and toward God.

In Flannery's letters, I find themes that are familiar to my native Reformed Christian clan: sin and grace. Fall and redemption. And the ultimate reality, God revealed in the incarnation. Flannery says other things, Catholic kinds of things I suppose, that I never heard in my Sunday school class. She calls for the abandonment of the self: "I measure God by everything I'm not." She embraces suffering, insisting that before grace can heal "it cuts with the sword Christ said he came to bring." While many casual believers think that faith is a big electric blanket, she says, of course it is a cross. Her Christian faith is a demanding one.

And then there's that word *mystery* again, one of her favorites. She never tosses it around in the way of fuzzy spirituality. Flannery's mystery is a rich and complex thing; it's the ground of her spiritual life, and it explains everything, though I'm still struggling to understand what she means by it. I do know what while we contemporary readers strip the cosmos of religious meaning, Flannery aims to return us to mystery, where the unseen ordering of the world speaks of God the Creator. "This is the central Christian mystery," Flannery says. "Life has, for all its horror, been found by God to be worth dying for."

❧ ❧ ❧

Nearly fifty years after Flannery's death, I hold a slender Sterling marbled composition book. It is Flannery's private prayer journal, written when she was nineteen years old and a student in Iowa. It's been recently discovered and published, complete with a facsimile of her own handwriting on lined pages.

"Dear God," the teenager begins in the first entry. "I cannot love Thee the way I want to. You are the slim crescent of a moon that I see and my self is the earth's shadow that keeps me from seeing all the moon." Flannery prays to know God. She asks to succeed with what she wants to do in the world. Flannery's journal is filled with questions. Will I ever know anything? How can I live—how shall I live? Can't anyone teach me how to pray? Am I keeping my faith out of laziness, dear God? Over the course of nearly two years, Flannery attends mass every morning, goes to class and privately journals her prayers, her battles, her hopes. At the last she blurts, "Oh Lord, make me a mystic, immediately."

In some journal entries, she prays for spiritual trust, for a clear mind, for a greater love for her holy Mother and for God, for the ones she loves. She prays for forgiveness. And then Flannery writes this one line, "Please help me to get down under things and find where You are."

Help me get down under things and find where You are. When I read her modest petition, I feel, at last, the meaning of mystery for Flannery. I may lay aside the scholarly editions of her fiction, the analytical essays, the underlined commentary. She has handed me a precious key to herself. She once said that fiction is the concrete expression of mystery—mystery that is lived. For Flannery, mystery is about getting down under things to find where God is, illuminating the divine foundation of all that is, seen and unseen.

Of all of O'Connor's writings, the words I'll remember best come from this yearning, young Flannery, the wavering believer who wrote, "I don't want to be doomed to mediocrity in my feeling for Christ. I want to feel. I want to love. Take me, dear Lord, and set me in the direction I am to go." In the pages of her journal, she reminds me of my high school self, the girl who grew up in the church, comfortable with its firm teachings and routines, yet who sensed a wildness beyond. Back then, when I was a teenager, Flannery found me, a disoriented, displaced Yankee, and she shook me up with shocking, hilarious, perplexing stories of the South—and of the Spirit. I want to keep on walking with Flannery: to feel, to love, to follow, to get down under things and find where God is.

Martin Luther 1483–1546

You Shall Not Die but Live!

Since the birds have learned so well the art of trusting Him
and of casting their cares from themselves upon God,
we who are his children should do so even more.

February has been icy and gray. As the fresh energies of a new semester fade, students pull me aside and tell me their fears: raw feelings about academic pressures, fragile relationships, and unnamed concerns. At least one out of every six young adults who walk through my door suffers from an anxiety disorder, the affliction of our age. I'm no therapist, that's for sure, but I know better than to blithely dispense words of good cheer. As we sit together, I listen intently and sometimes offer a "Counseling Resources in Charlottesville" handout. I wonder if it makes any difference.

Another blizzard brings two hours of shoveling; plans are cancelled. As the work piles up and winter wears on, I grow uneasy in my skin. I crave some warm sunshine. My imagination runs to and fro as I rehearse family conflicts and looming deadlines. Then I move on to darker visions of war, global poverty, environmental alarms, political unrest. Disquiet visits my heart, whispering that things have never been bleaker. Who else knows how I feel?

❧ ❧ ❧

Martin Luther experienced angst in the extreme. Born five hundred years ago into a humble copper miner's family, it was neither career uncertainty nor economic worry that most troubled young Martin, though I'll bet that German winter got him down. Martin experienced distress of cosmic dimensions. He was petrified by death, hell, and the avenging wrath of God. At twenty years old, weeping and wailing, trembling and doubting, Martin despaired over the salvation of his own soul. He was convinced that God's grace was utterly blocked by his mortal guilt and that there was just no way out. "To cry unto the Lord, that is beyond us," he lamented, "for our bad conscience and our sin press down on us, and lie so about our necks so badly that we feel the Wrath of God: and the whole world could not be so heavy as that burden."

The Jesus of Martin's imagination promised no refuge; he never showed up as a brotherly Savior offering comfort. When Martin kneeled on the stone floor of the unheated church, the young man looked up to the crucifix with the suffering Christ hanging there—and he saw a harsh judge from whom he wanted to flee. Martin turned pale, terrified by the very name of Jesus; Christ's accusing gaze was, he said, a lightning stroke to him.

But one day, Martin was caught out in an open field during a violent thunderstorm, convinced that a fiery death was at hand. In desperation he cried out for rescue and vowed to become a monk if only God would spare his life. Martin survived the storm. I've also made some impulsive, emergency promises, bargaining with God and then always managing to forget, but Martin actually made good on his prayer. He gave away his possessions and signed on at the Augustinian monastery before even checking with his parents. They'd been pushing him to become a respectable lawyer. Eager to go all the way, Martin, at twenty-four, became a priest.

Unfortunately, Martin's new religious vocation provided zero relief from his anxiety. Martin found no peace within the monastery walls despite his scrupulous regimen of vigils, fasts, confessions, and grueling self-punishments. Plagued by unhapiness, he was tormented by the vision of an irate God who set impossibly high standards then damned him for failing to achieve them. Martin came to hate the God he was commanded to serve.

Disillusioned, melancholy Martin lost all hope in the church's claims to salvation. The corruption of the medieval church, with its pay-your-way-to-heaven scams, pushed him over the edge. On October 31, 1517, Martin nailed his famous protest declaration, his Ninety-Five Theses, onto the massive door of the Castle Church in Wittenberg, declaring war against the Christian establishment. With that, the Protestant Reformation began.

Martin antagonized the church elites and then stubbornly refused to recant. The authorities excommunicated him as a heretic, vowing fatal penalties. Martin, a convicted clerical outlaw on the lam, hid out behind the walls of Wartburg Castle for almost a year.

Driven by rebellion and despair, Martin turned to the Bible. Paul's words in Romans captured his attention: "'He who through faith is righteous shall live" (Romans 1:17). With that revelation, everything changed. Martin was released from his doomed efforts to win God's pleasure, the impasse of church dogma and religious piety. Faith, he realized, is simple trust in God's promises, no matter how we feel or what we accomplish. What an unexpected, astounding truth: salvation is a gift! In a profound emotional rush, Martin declared, "When I realized this, I felt myself born again." It was as if "the gates of paradise had been flung open" and he'd walked in.

Did Martin's newfound spiritual freedom heal his heart and calm him down? Hardly.

Intense, complex Martin launched ferocious doctrinal debates and waged personal battles. Unwilling to back down, Luther vilified his opponents as dragons, specters and witches, monsters of perdition, and enemies in a pantheon of wickedness. (You did not want to get on this guy's bad side.) Martin's countercultural ideas took off and ignited violent peasant uprisings. Historians say that his theological revolution ushered in the modern era of Western history. So, uh, no. Martin never calmed down.

Martin did find some pleasure in human love. No longer a monk in good standing, Martin Luther married Katharina von Bora, a runaway nun. She'd escaped the fortifications of her convent hidden in an empty fish barrel, a display of her innovative spirit. Katharina was one no-nonsense wife. She ran a buzzing household, supervised their six children, hosted mobs of relations and theology students, and all while she managed her brewery, vegetable garden, and fish hatchery. It's no wonder Martin utterly adored the woman. He warmly announced, "There is no more lovely, friendly, and charming relationship, communion, or company than a good marriage."

Even with intimate family affection, close community, prayer, biblical conviction, and outsized courage, Martin was still plagued by chronic anxiety to the end of his life, a condition he named *Anfechtung*, with its connotation of assault. At fifty, Luther lamented that his dark emotional afflictions, those "weapons of death," were still troubling him—more worrisome than any of his intellectual labors or personal enemies. One strategy usually helped. When things got bad, he said, he got into bed and embraced his Katy until her nearness sent the demonic depressions away.

In Martin's time, fellow sufferers came to him and begged for counsel. Pastor Martin first responded with scriptural insights. Jesus knows that we worry, he truly does, Martin assured them (and us). So listen deeply to Jesus' words, he'd say: "Let not your hearts be troubled. Trust in God." In your hopelessness, your angst, your helplessness, there is a clear divine command: Rejoice! Yes, Martin, insists, "The Christian should and must be a cheerful person." I for one read this and ask: isn't cheerfulness a lot to expect? I know I can hardly complain, compared to some impoverished Germanic peasant in the year 1500. But still. I can't just put on a happy face.

It's no secret that Martin knew, from personal experience, that it can be tough to rejoice; he's preaching to himself more than anyone. Once he's made his theological point, Martin goes on to offer a range of practical pastoral strategies, concrete recommendations that fill his letters of spiritual counseling. Here are my top five picks.

Remind yourself of the resurrection reality of Jesus. Tell yourself the gospel truth until you believe it. Repeat out loud and often, "I shall not die but live! I shall not die but live! I shall not die but live!" The sixteenth-century version of a positive affirmation.

Don't spend too much time by yourself, where "the worst and saddest things come to mind." Martin knows that when we're alone "we imagine that other people are very happy, and it distresses us that things go well with them and evil with us." (I'm certain he'd agree that hours on social media make it even worse.) Instead, he urges, seek the company and comfort of others. Be merry with them, for gladness and good cheer are the best medicine.

Get active. Martin makes numerous suggestions here. Engage in riding and hunting, he tells a despondent young prince. Play music and sing a joyful song to the Lord. Harness the horse and spread manure on the fields. Eat and drink with abandon. Joke, for the devil hates gaiety, he says. Play games, practice sports. Following his own advice, Martin builds a single-lane bowling alley in his own house.

Read the biblical stories of faithful people who suffered too. People like Noah and his family, who were shut up in the ark for so long. Martin envisions them enduring endless masses of rain, tossed about by waves, simply adrift. Don't you know they wondered if God loved or even remembered them? he asks. Though their hardships were grave, God saved them in the end. Take hope in their salvation.

Call upon the Lord. (See Psalm 118.) Prayer is the one thing you absolutely cannot do without. "You must learn to call," Luther writes. "Do not sit by yourself or lie on a couch, hanging and shaking your head letting your thoughts torture you." Don't brood about your terrible life, how miserable you feel, and what a bad person you are. Instead, tell yourself, "Get a grip on yourself, you lazy bum!" Luther goes on. Fall on your knees, and raise your hands and eyes toward heaven. Read a psalm. Say the Lord's Prayer, tell God what you need. Lay your anxiety down before God and listen for God's voice, that you will truly know the confidence of God's mercy.

It is said that Martin prayed the Lord's Prayer eight times a day. I don't think he did it as an act of rote religiosity. Instead, I think Martin was daily tested by his apprehension, continually forced back to ask for God's help. Only in prayer was Martin assured, as he said, that Christ loved him, that the Father loved him, that the Holy Spirit loved him.

❧ ❧ ❧

I imagine going back to sixteenth-century Wittenberg for an afternoon. I walk along Collegienstrasse and through the Katharinenportal to enter the Luther-Von Bora house. I pull a chair up to the heavy wooden table in the Lutherstube and join the men for several hours of heated intellectual debate. In the courtyard, the Luther kids scramble after squawking chickens beyond the smoky kitchen. The chatter, the commotion, the conflict. It's just too much. I have to get outside and walk.

Katharina and Martin guide me into the medieval streets. We push through the crowded market square, past crofters' clay and straw huts, through the ramparts and city gate and into the open summer fields of Saxony. Here, with the sun on our faces, Martin drops his cantankerous tone for a more pastoral, reflective manner.

Martin quotes Jesus, who said, "Do not be anxious, saying 'What shall we eat?' or 'What shall we drink?' or 'What shall we wear?' Your heavenly Father knows that you need these things." As we amble through the grass, I picture Martin as the young man who bolted across this very meadow, caught in the stormy terror of God's wrath. Here he is, speaking of grace. I know that it's not easy for him.

Katharina points out the osprey overhead and the glowing scarlet poppies along the path. God feeds and nourishes everything that lives. Walking for miles out here, I think I'm feeling better. I let go of my mental wrangling long enough to hear the songs of the birds around me, the thrushes, blackbirds, and linnets. The goldfinch, feathered in brilliant chrome yellow and glistening black, is a winged theologian that sings God's provident praise.

Refreshed, I feel that I can return to my own life, to my young friends who are so overcome by worry, in need of counsel. I'll stay vigilant for the warning signs of real trouble: prolonged sadness, excessive distress or panic, isolation, self-harm, even talk of suicide—and willingly go alongside them to find professional care. At other times, we'll struggle on together. The words of Scripture and prayer, walks in the garden and on the trail, hours of play and conversation, will confirm in us God's enduring, unfailing love.

Amanda Berry Smith 1837–1915

Lean In, Lean On

Then I saw what was the matter. Fear!

OUR DAUGHTER, NAN, will be on her way—off to college and then, so soon, out into what we call *real life*. As Nan chooses her major and considers a vocation, Facebook executive Sheryl Sandberg has strong advice for her: "Have the ambition to lean in to your career and run the world." Sandberg challenges gifted young women like Nan to step up. Lead the way. Aim for the top. Transform society. "The world needs you to change it," Sandberg declares in her book *Lean In*. "Women all around the world are counting on you."

If I'd heard those words at Nan's age, I would have panicked. The women of the world are depending on *me*?! I got my liberal arts degree, collected my diploma, and moved the stuff out of my student apartment—with no idea where to begin. Facing adulthood, I felt disoriented and unsure about what exactly I could "lean in" to. I ended up at a high-end toy store where I stacked handcrafted alphabet blocks and sold intellectually stimulating toys to parents angling to improve their drooling infants' Harvard admission prospects. In high-rise offices, ambitious women made deals in 1980s power suits with shoulder pads. Downstairs, I vacuumed trampled Goldfish crackers for $3.35 an hour and pondered my next move.

Sheryl Sandberg issues one final charge: "Please ask yourself: What would I do if I weren't afraid? And then go do it." Decades after my own college graduation, this tantalizing query follows me as I consider my meandering way from toy store to grad school to teaching to ministry. Does fear hold me back from my deepest calling—or even from daily acts of courage? What would I do if I weren't afraid? I wonder.

What would you do if you weren't afraid? It would seem a cruel question to ask of Amanda Berry Smith, born into slavery, desperate poverty, danger, racism, and misogyny; she had every good reason to be afraid. Yet through her fear, Amanda Berry Smith leaned fully into God's power and presence. She stood up, trembling, and preached the gospel to people of all races. She traveled the world as an evangelist. She was a woman who knew what it took to change the world—and she did it.

Amanda began life in captivity in 1837. Her father, Samuel Berry, enslaved on a neighboring Maryland farm, made brooms late into the night to purchase his family's freedom. They moved across the border to York, Pennsylvania, where the Berry house was a station of the Underground Railroad. One night, slave trackers burst in; they beat up Samuel and stabbed Amanda's mother. When freeborn sister Frances went to visit an aunt in Maryland, she was captured and sold. Somehow Amanda earned the fifty dollars to buy Frances back.

Amanda, with only three months of formal education, tells her story in an autobiography, *The Story of the Lord's Dealings with Mrs. Amanda Smith, the Colored Evangelist: Containing an Account of Her Life Work of Faith, and Her Travels in America, England, Ireland, Scotland, India, and Africa as an Independent Missionary.* (You can't buy it at your local bookseller, so save yourself the trip. Smith's memoir might be lost forever if it weren't for the online archives of the University of North Carolina.)

Reading Amanda's obscure book, we get an inside look at a vulnerable woman's life of privation, hunger, ill health, and intense stress. She barely survives the rigors of manual labor, sweating over laundry for only pennies a day. Amanda endures two disastrous marriages. She grieves the early deaths of four of her five children; when her son Willy dies simply for lack of medicine, she doesn't have the twenty dollars for his funeral. Amanda speaks frankly of her constant struggles with fear. "I always had a fear of white people," she writes, a trepidation borne out in daily experiences of prejudice. In Amanda's telling, it is the doing of Satan at her side, hissing words of self-doubt, deception, and distress. Satan brings the cold dread that holds her captive.

What would you do if you weren't afraid? Above security or health, young Amanda desperately desires to experience the immediate, living power of God. She leans in to receive the Spirit and makes a daring vow, "I will pray once more, and if there is any such thing as salvation, I am determined to have it this afternoon or die." In church one day, she receives, at her core, the sanctifying presence of the Holy. She describes the feeling: wonderfully strange yet glorious. She feels a hand, ineffable, press gently on her head. A power moves, rolls down, and covers her like a great cloak.

Amanda's spiritual encounter leaves her feeling elated, gentled, peaceful, and powerful. As soon as the ecstatic young woman leaves the church, fear threatens her newfound joy. There ahead of her are three leading sisters from her church, promenading up Green Street as if all godly wisdom dwells with them. As Amanda approaches, they whisper together. Are those respectable church ladies gossiping about her? Will Amanda approach them to declare the glorious things that God has just done?

She hears the devil mocking her timidity and, shaken, she falters. Then, unexpectedly, God surprises her with boldness. I love how Amanda tells the story: "I don't know why, but O I felt mighty, as I came near those sisters." Unashamed, Amanda blurts out the good news: the Lord has sanctified my soul! The women are speechless as Amanda strides on by, swinging her arm like a boy. Amanda writes, "I suppose the people thought I was wild, and I was, for God had set me on fire! 'O,' I thought, 'if there was a platform around the world I would be willing to get on it and walk and tell everybody of this sanctifying power of God!'"

From that day forward, Amanda was propelled by passion for two things: to know God and to tell others about him. At that time, women were not welcome in pulpits, and certainly not black women. But in a vision, Amanda saw two fiery letters spelling out the command GO. So she preached and sang, dressed plainly in black, gray, and white. Church ladies couldn't silence her anymore.

Amanda recounts her troubles with the formidable Brother Turpin, a fierce minister who opposed her public preaching. In anticipation of Sunday's worship service, she was laid low by worry. Amanda spent a Friday in fasting and prayer, though Satan tormented her with discouraging accusations. At 2:00 that afternoon, she took her Bible and knelt down. "Oh! Lord, show me what is the matter. Why is this darkness in my mind?" she prayed. The Spirit directed her to read and Amanda recalls, "I opened my Bible, and my eyes lighted on these words: 'Perfect love casteth out fear. He that feareth has not been made perfect in love.' Then I saw what was the matter. Fear!"

* * *

Fear. Yes, fear is the matter. So what am I afraid of? I tear off a sheet of notebook paper and begin to scribble. I'm afraid of illness, weakness, of getting old. I'm afraid to lose my husband or my children. I'm afraid to give up my financial security and my comfortable home. I'm afraid of what other people think of me, of their disapproval or hurt feelings. I'm afraid to ask for what I want. I'm afraid to take risks.

I'm making good headway on my fear list until I glimpse myself through Amanda's eyes. I see an advantaged, educated, healthy, accomplished twenty-first-century white woman in possession of a family, a career, and a Volvo station wagon. In that moment I am deeply ashamed of my fear. Compared to Amanda's, mine looks a whole lot like indulgent selfishness. I sit with that feeling.

What would you do if you weren't afraid? Amanda was called to preach but she was terrified, and for good reason. So she prayed for help: "Oh! Lord, . . . give me complete victory over this fear." The answer came in silence. Circumstances didn't change and there was no "especial manifestation," but Amanda had a deep sense that God had delivered her—and she praised him.

When God took Amanda's fear away, God also called her to take action—to testify at Union Church. Amanda replied, "Yes, Lord, if Thou wilt help me, and give me Thy strength, and go with me, I will go." And so on Sunday, after a "mighty skimpey" breakfast, Amanda showed up, ready to face a congregation of skeptical strangers. The presiding elder announced her with a sarcastic joke: "Mrs. Smith is from New York; she *says* the Lord sent her." Amanda remembers, "Oh, my heart fell down, and I said, 'Oh! Lord, help. Give me the message.'"

Amanda was trembling from head to foot. She didn't even know what verse she'd preach about; she was waiting on God for that, and time was running out. When the moment arrived for her to exhort, Amanda quaked so badly that even the pastor, sitting next to her at the pulpit, saw it. She heard him say, "Now, my child, you needn't be afraid. Lean on the Lord. He will help you."

Lean in and lean on the God who is near. I notice that Amanda did not muster her own rhetorical skills or dig deep for self-confidence. She was out on the ledge with God alone. Before the packed house she stood up, heart pounding. Amanda told of how the Lord gave her great liberty in preaching as her fright melted away. "I seemed to lose sight of everybody and everything but my responsibility to God and my duty to the people. The Holy Ghost fell on the people and we had a wonderful time. Souls were convicted and some converted that night."

Through controversy and hardship, Amanda Berry Smith, the self-taught former slave, a woman of color, became known as an evangelist. She traveled across oceans and around the world, a preacher unlike any the people had seen before. Whenever she spoke in England and Scotland, as many as six hundred people came out. In Calcutta, where angry protestors threatened violence, Amanda knelt down on the grass and prayed until the crowd fell silent. She visited schools and mission stations through Liberia, traveling by canoe, suffering malaria. Back in the United States, she founded an orphanage for African American girls. She preached and labored till her death at seventy-eight, answering the *what would you do* question with her very life.

❧ ❧ ❧

But I still haven't answered my own questions, have I? Are women all around the world really counting on me? And what *would* I do if I weren't afraid?

As to the women of the world, let's hope their well-being is beyond me. It would be silly arrogance to claim big answers to my gender's pressing quandaries. But just as I brush that one off, I think of my daughter, Nan. My mother. My nieces. I imagine dozens of female students, women near me in church, the women I touch in ways I don't even imagine. Where could I lead the way, for their sake?

As to my fears, Nan's a sharp observer, and she's on to me. She sees me try to avoid fear. Dismiss it, play it down, and even dress it up with a gold bracelet stamped with the word *fearless*. She'd laugh if I seriously tried repeating aloud the 15 Affirmations for Anxiety to Help Calm Yourself that I found online. She'd see right through mantras like "I overcome my fear of anything and everything and live life courageously." Or "Fear is no match for my strong spirit and will." I think Nan is relying on me to be honest about my fear and, in my best moments, turn to God for the strength to do hard things.

In our very different times and places, Amanda and I are two sisters in a long line of fearful people. If we met up after one of her sermons, Amanda just might grip my arm and say, "Now, my child, you needn't be afraid. Lean on the Lord. He will help you."

So what would I do if I weren't afraid? That turns out to be a trick question. What will I do *through* my fear, even when my legs are quaking? That's more like it. I will ask God to let me live with grace when I'm weak. With trust when I lose treasured people and precious possessions. With generosity when others need my time and my gifts. With courage to speak my mind clearly. And more than anything, I will ask God for the strong love that casts out fear.

Dietrich Bonhoeffer 1906–1945

Live Unreservedly, Grounded in God

Who am I? They mock me, these lonely questions of mine.

Whoever I am, Thou knowest, O God, I am thine!

The heavy wooden doors creak as I step into the chapel this Monday morning; I'm late again. In the distant realms of grownups and schoolchildren, the day began long ago. Most college kids are still deep in sleep, catching up after a festive weekend. The only sounds are of university buses idling outside, leaf blowers clearing the sidewalks and an ancient heater wheezing in the basement. Within the Victorian stone chapel, jeweled light filters through stained glass and spills onto the floor where Reilly, Maddy, Cameron, and Betty have settled down to pray. Cameron picks up his guitar and we sing, "O Lord, let my soul rise up to meet you as the day rises to meet the sun."

These students, who've come here willingly, pray with open hearts, fervent in their belief and honest in their confessions. They look to me as a mentor who will lead them into a deeper spiritual life. An older sister in faith—wise, solid, calm. But my soul does not rise up to the Lord, not at all. Who am I? In the silence, the question comes to me. What am I doing here? On this day I cannot pray. My mind traces its cycle of worries. There's a feeling of sorrow in my gut. Empty. Lost.

Planted here on the carpet, my own darkness and distraction lingers. If I could say just anything to the friends in this circle, it might be this: "I realize that you think highly of me. But I'm not who you think I am."

I read aloud the words of the liturgy and hear them echo against the granite walls. Our reading today is from Dietrich Bonhoeffer: "At the threshold of the new day stands the Lord who made it. All the darkness and distraction of the dreams of night retreat before the clear light of Jesus Christ and His wakening word." Where is that clear light of Jesus Christ? I'd like to be more like Dietrich, a Christian hero, the German theologian and pastor who opposed Hitler. He stood up for righteousness and paid the ultimate price when he was executed by the Nazis in 1945. I stand in awe of the man. In the morning quiet, I ponder whether Dietrich ever doubted himself. How would he, expected to be strong, know anything of my faltering spirit?

Dietrich had nerve. Only twenty-seven years old, he discerned the Nazi danger early on. Within two days of Adolf Hitler's rise to power as chancellor in 1933, Dietrich delivered a radio address repudiating the führer's perverse promises to the German people. Ten minutes into the broadcast, he was cut off in mid-sentence. It wasn't long before the young troublemaker was officially silenced on account of his challenges to Hitler.

Dietrich was convinced that Christ had called him to act, so in 1935 he created Finkenwalde, an illegal seminary for dissident Protestant preachers. On a secluded seaside estate on the northern Baltic coast, the seminary may have seemed isolated from the firestorm engulfing Germany, but the community was no self-contained, pious retreat from the world; it was a daring demonstration of Christian countercultural witness.

The small experiment in what Dietrich called "new monasticism" was designed to strengthen the seminarians at a time when living according to Jesus' Sermon on the Mount was a hazardous venture. Even as news came of dissenting pastors threatened, arrested, imprisoned, and forced into the army, the underground seminarians persisted in daily prayer, worship, work, and study.

What does it mean to be a Christian today? Dietrich never stopped pressing this vital question. In a time of crisis, he said, "Everything depends on the urgent invitation to take the first step into what is still an unknown, a new situation." Dietrich went to the Bible in search of answers. He assigned the students a biblical text and instructed them to pray over the passage, to see their own lives in its light.

Life at Finkenwalde was not 24/7 spiritual discipline. It had its physical pleasures too. Dietrich organized recreation in the sunshine, hotly contested tennis matches, hikes in the forest, bracing plunges into the Baltic Sea. Evenings at Finkenwalde were spent around the piano, singing hymns and the Negro spirituals Dietrich learned in Harlem during his studies in America.

Christian community comes alive in Dietrich's *Life Together*, the slim volume that's become a classic, a spiritual instruction manual for Christians building their own intentional fellowships. The brothers shared everything—coffee, labor, and Ping-Pong, meditation, prayer, and Scripture—and discovered that the very physical presence of other Christians proved a source of incomparable joy and strength. Sadly, by the time Dietrich penned those words, the seminary had been torn apart, shut down by the Gestapo. As Dietrich wrote *Life Together*, the friends' life together was a thing of the past, a poignant meditation on all that was lost.

After experiencing the "lightning flash of eternity," the beauty that is true Christian community, loneliness lay ahead for Dietrich. The Nazis barred him from preaching and speaking in public; he was fired from his teaching post at the University of Berlin, and Finkenwalde was shuttered by the Gestapo. More and more, Dietrich's convictions cost him his friendships and his freedom.

Many of us know Dietrich's story. He wouldn't back down under pressure. He held fast to the conviction that his allegiance to Christ demanded resistance to the Third Reich; without it, he could not claim to be a true Christian. In the face of radical evil, the pacifist pastor made a radical choice: he joined the conspiracy to assassinate Hitler. Many have wondered how he justified the move from peace to violence. There are times when both the no and the yes involve guilt, Dietrich said. It is then, in those tough decisions, that we must believe that, whatever we do, our guilt is carried by Christ.

Dietrich sought to understand God's will in the here and now—to the very end. In public he appeared bravely assured, even when his Christian faith took him far out into the world and, ultimately, to imprisonment by the Nazis. In the two years between his arrest and his death, Dietrich never stopped writing. Prayers, poems, Scripture studies, theological fragments, book ideas. Personal letters to his family and to his friend and soulmate, Eberhard Bethge. Dietrich's writings brim with creative intelligence, warm love, and, always, reliance on God.

From cell number twenty-five in Tegel prison, Dietrich continued to marvel at "how beautiful this world can be." The glimpse of a few colorful flowers, the verdant linden tree in the prison yard, brought back a phrase of poetry: "Still is the world, this gorgeous world entirely resilient." Even during the worst days, Dietrich returned to hymns, memories, prayers, psalms, novels, poetry, and beloved scholarly texts. The Moravian daily prayer book of his childhood anchored Dietrich in Scripture and nourished his soul in the midst of distress.

Dietrich wrote to his distraught parents, to reassure them of his well-being in confinement, yet in private letters to Eberhard he described his suffering. He conceded that "despite everything that I have written, it is horrible here." There were times when our courageous saint confessed that he found the world "a nauseating burden." His private journal reveals even darker scribblings of despair and resignation.

In prison, Dietrich penned a deeply personal poem. In it I hear the echo of my unspoken thoughts, the doubts I feel as I sit on the chapel floor for morning prayer. "Who am I?" he begins. Dietrich considers first what other people think of him: "They often tell me I stepped from my cell's confinement calmly, cheerfully, firmly, like a squire from his country house." Even his warders admired Dietrich's equanimity, his friendliness. They see a confident man, "one accustomed to win."

"Am I then really that which other men tell of?" Dietrich asks himself. His brave public persona is so different from the man he knows himself to be. The man who is restless, longing, sick, like a bird in a cage. Struggling for breath, thirsty for kindness, yearning for beauty. Alone, Dietrich longs for friends who remain "at an infinite distance." He is weary and empty at praying and thinking. Ready to say farewell to it all, he admits.

I marvel at the depth of Dietrich's spirit, even after all he'd been through and with every reason to abandon hope. From early on, he chose to put himself into God's hands and to live "unreservedly in life's duties, problems, successes and failures, experiences and perplexities." To live *unreservedly*. (My heart leaps at the thought.) Years of morning meditation, crossing the threshold of each day in prayer, prepared Dietrich to see by the clear light of Jesus Christ. Days of disciplined study gave him ears to hear the powerful, wakening word—the Word that speaks salvation, redemption, love. Dietrich's everyday devotional practices were energized by living obedience. For him, prayer required response and influenced his tasks, decisions, sins, and temptations. When dark doubts churned within him, Dietrich remained grounded in God's faithfulness.

And who am I? People will tell you that I'm an energetic woman, caring, composed, reliable. They see a loyal wife, an affectionate mother, a trustworthy friend. Out in the world I'm known as a person of sincere and warm-hearted faith who speaks of God with assurance and prays in a strong voice.

The horrors of the Third Reich are in a world far removed from my own; I enjoy a privileged life. Yet even in my freedom, surrounded by people I love and the work that I enjoy, I know myself to be restless too. Dietrich describes the gasp for air, the hand compressing his throat. That inner struggle is real to me. The chill voices of misgiving tell me that I am weak, a doubter, no authentic Christian. They murmur that I'm a hypocrite for letting people assume that my faith is sturdy when inside I'm shaky. How reliable are these accusing messages? Does my inner critic speak the truth of who I am?

In his poem, Dietrich returns to this question "Who am I?" I read on as my own anxious petitions press in upon me. Dietrich concludes with the lines "They mock me, these lonely questions of mine. Whoever I am, Thou knowest, O God, I am thine!" With a shift into prayer, Dietrich gently turns me around. Away from myself and toward God. God, the one who knows who I really am, beyond others' assumptions and my own judgments. God knows who I am. *I am God's*. What more do I need to know?

Thanks to Reilly, Maddy, Cameron, and Betty, I got myself to the chapel this early morning. As I look into their faces now, I am newly mindful that, as Dietrich said, the precious time that separates us from utter loneliness may be brief indeed. Throughout the world today, other Christians are torn apart by conflict, by circumstances beyond their control. As we sit together on the floor, we pray for those believers and acknowledge, with thanks, that "it is grace, nothing but grace, that we are allowed to live in community with Christian brethren."

As for me, I rest in the affection of friends and in an assurance of God's love that resounds in the steadying words of ancient prayers. A word from the gospel to sustain me for the day to come. And so we say our amens, push open the heavy chapel doors, and step out into the dazzling world of spring, held in the arms of God.

A. W. Tozer 1897–1963

Pursue True Blessedness

In the matter of faith, I was completely alone. . . .
By the grace of God, I stood alone and I have always
been able to thank God for the results.

Born in 1894, intelligent Betty Sweet was college educated and she made the most of her domestic science major: she kept a gracious, well-ordered household, was committed to her church and her family, and prepared homemade cinnamon applesauce and fragrant strawberry rhubarb pie with fruit from my grandfather's abundant garden. Betty wore perfectly pressed dresses, support stockings, and practical shoes, her hair carefully arranged at all times.

A serious teacher of Scripture, my grandmother woke before dawn to pray and study in her corner breakfast nook, filling her Bible with detailed marginalia. When one leather-bound volume could hold no more of her penciled notations, Betty bought another Bible and began again.

Betty also taught a community Bible study that caused a bit of a stir when prominent businessmen came to study "under" her. Family lore recounts how the town's male pastors appealed, without success, to my grandfather to stop his wife from her impertinent practice. Growing up under the influence of Betty's thoroughgoing efficiency and spiritual devotion, I was both admiring and intimidated.

❧ ❧ ❧

As a young girl, I heard about Pastor Aiden W. Tozer from my grandmother, who traveled great distances to hear his dynamic Bible exposition. My grandmother's favorite text was *The Pursuit of God*, a book that Aiden composed by hand, all in one night. She told the story of how he boarded an evening train in Chicago and took his seat with only pen, paper, and a Bible. Inspired, he began to write, with the words coming as fast as he could scribble. When Aiden stepped out onto the sunny railway platform in McAllan, Texas, *The Pursuit of God* was complete. Like Betty, Aiden spoke with the voice of a wholly committed soul thirsting after God, one who literally burns the midnight oil to know the Holy One.

This great Aiden W. Tozer was a child of poverty; he had no formal education, and he never went to seminary. Aiden came early to his life of discipline. His character was formed by a hardscrabble childhood of subsistence farming in Pennsylvania's Allegheny mountains. Catastrophe came when fire consumed the Tozers' home. His father, Jacob, became incapacitated by deep depression, so ten-year-old Aiden took on the burdens of the farm and family.

At fifteen, Aiden moved to industrial Akron, Ohio, and took a menial job at the B. F. Goodrich tire factory. Walking back from work one day, Aiden stopped to listen to a street-corner preacher with a simple message: if you don't know how to be saved, just call on God for mercy. Aiden recalls, "I was little better than a pagan but with only that kind of skimpy biblical background, I became greatly disturbed, for I began to feel and sense and acknowledge God's gracious Presence." Aiden, who had not been raised in the church, went home, climbed up into the attic and there, all by himself, gave his life to Jesus Christ. His first closet prayer.

For the rest of his life, the self-sufficient country boy would always seek out God on his own. When Aiden showed up in church one

Sunday, a bright teenager named Ada Pfautz noticed this aloneness. She later recalled that Aiden, being only a beginner in the faith and with little schooling, was dependent on the Lord entirely.

The two married young, convinced that God had called him to preach, though the nineteen-year-old bride fretted over Aiden's poor English ("pure Pennsylvaniaish"), his outmoded high-top dress shoes and cheap haircuts. They spent their last dollars on train tickets to West Virginia, where Aiden led his first revival meetings.

Aiden's knowledge increased quickly as he devoured all of the classic Christian texts and Bible commentaries he could get. His Bible, his reading, his prayer time, and his preaching fueled a theology not of the head but of the heart. Aiden Tozer's reputation as an evangelist and a preacher grew, though his fashion sense didn't improve one bit.

As for social graces, he wouldn't bother. Aiden had no interest in making a good impression. He saw himself as a prophet, not a diplomat. There would be no small talk with parishioners after church services. (Tozer slipped away to the nursery to see the toddlers.) He refused to do counseling, pastoral or hospital visits; he left that to other, flashier pastors. On his first Sunday as the new minister of a Chicago church, Aiden got up into the pulpit, said not a word about being pleased to be there, skipped the niceties, and started right in on the eleventh chapter of Hebrews.

Even on the day of his ordination, Tozer left the reception in his honor to hide out in his study. While the guests nibbled cookies and drank punch, he made no apologies for meeting his Savior in secret. "The Prayer of a Minor Prophet," which he composed that day, reveals his heart: "Save me from the bondage to things. Let me not waste my days puttering around the house." He speaks of ministry as sacrifice: "Lay Thy terror upon me, O God, and drive me to the place of prayer. . . . Deliver me from overeating and late sleeping. Teach me self-discipline that I may be a good soldier of Jesus Christ."

Every morning Aiden secluded himself in his office, hung up his suit trousers, put on his raggedy old "prayer pants," and lay facedown on the floor to worship God, oblivious to the world. Aiden's undisturbed, solitary, closet prayer times lasted for hours. Those long daily sessions in tattered prayer pants took Aiden deep into intense conversation with God. He never gave it up, even as the needs of his growing family and his flourishing ministry expanded. Intimacy with God was everything to him.

The audiences who flocked to hear Aiden preach marveled that he had a sacred anointing, said that he had been with Jesus. Over the years, Aiden was renowned for declaring that he had no regard for money. Many admired this devout man who disdained ungodly mammon and creature comforts. What did financial security have to do with the pursuit of God? Nothing!

Why did Aiden care so little about material things? In his essay "The Blessedness of Possessing Nothing," he begins at the beginning. At creation, God made a world of useful, pleasant things for human sustenance and delight. God was sovereign within our hearts, and we freely enjoyed God's bountiful gifts. Then sin arrived and turned things upside down; our trouble started when we chose to revere "things" over God. God's creation, made for our good, became a source of ruin to our souls.

Aiden perceives why there is only fear and discontent in our hearts: we're controlled by a tyranny of things. Possessions, ambition, even beloved family and friends, come before God. Aiden calls us to relinquish our treasures and put God back in the center of our lives. Only then, praising God above everything, will we know joy and inner freedom.

❧ ❧ ❧

I'll give it to Aiden Tozer. He practiced what he preached. Even after he became a successful pastor, a prolific writer, and a popular evangelist, he kept to his extreme version of the "keep it simple" philosophy.

Aiden rejected salary increases and had a habit of donating half of his salary back to the church. He gave away book royalties and paychecks. He never even bought a car. When he died in 1963, his gravestone read only "A Man of God."

Though he cared nothing for money or pleasure, Aiden poured passionate, unbounded energy into teaching the biblical "deeper life" to audiences of adoring college students and thoughtful followers like Betty Sweet. But Aiden's family hungered for some of that emotional engagement.

Aiden rarely played with his seven kids and never once planned a family vacation, for he was utterly indifferent to leisure. Finally, after decades of asking for a holiday, Aiden's youngest daughter, Becca, recruited a friend to drive her and her parents on their first vacation, a trip to the Smoky Mountains. Aiden, almost sixty years old by then, groused the whole way.

It is simple enough to revere a preacher who's just too spiritual to care for things of this world. But as a mother and a wife, my mind goes to the practical things; I imagine the great man from his family's point of view. Longsuffering Ada and the Tozer children bore the hard consequences of Aiden's asceticism. Even as her husband gave away half of his salary, Ada could barely clothe and feed the growing kids (who grew up to despise macaroni). Because her thrifty husband refused to invest in a car, Mrs. Tozer was forced to beg rides and walk long distances in the freezing Chicago winters. Lowell, the oldest child, remarked sardonically that his mother was a single parent.

Out of public view, both Aiden and Ada lived with depression. One daughter remembers her mother as a sad woman who struggled to be cheerful, to be a more "godly" wife who could give up her own desires. Ada herself once said, "My husband was so close to God, a man of such deep prayer, always on his knees, that he could not communicate with me or our family." Even Aiden once admitted his private isolation to another pastor, confiding, "I've had a lonely life."

After her husband's death, Ada learned that Aiden had relinquished the rights to all income on his best-selling books. He had rejected his church's provisions for a pension fund. She'd been left with nothing. A year after Aiden died, Ada married Leonard Odam, an older widower—a man who owned a car and taught her to drive! Ada told friends, "I have never been happier in my life. Aiden loved Jesus Christ, but Leonard Odam loves me."

❧ ❧ ❧

I think I understand why my grandmother always admired A. W. Tozer's unreserved commitment to personal communion with God. She meditated on his penetrating, insightful writing and his fearless sermons. Here was a man unencumbered by the quest for fame or fortune, living simply and freely, sustained by God alone. But when I read his words on the blessedness of possessing nothing, I envision the faces of people who suffered for his high mindedness.

I imagine Ada, the wife of forty-five years, alone in her marriage to a preoccupied man, impoverished at his death. I think of the seven children who went unnoticed by their father, the iconic preacher secluded in his office, praying on the floor in his prayer pants and extolling the "lonely valleys of soul poverty and abnegation of all things." Ada and her children never experienced Aiden's personal sense of blessedness, and that breaks my heart. It makes me furious.

What do I do with Betty's fallen spiritual hero? For my devoted grandmother's sake, I'm looking for a way to think well of him. So here's where I start. I've heard a saint described as "a sinner, writ large," someone who struggles exceptionally hard to turn a bad thing into a good one. Aiden certainly struggled and sinned, so by that definition, he just may qualify. A saint is not perfect, I get that. Even people who are redeemed by Christ still live in the world—and they carry (and inflict) scars, pains, weaknesses. If I can gather up some compassion, even a measure of humility, I may learn something of spiritual value from Aiden without liking him in the least.

Aiden's message to me is singular and ardent: to know God is my greatest purpose. When possessions, status, and distractions capture my worshiping heart, then I am bound to suffer. Aiden promises that an intimate and satisfying knowledge of God is waiting for me if only I will come to God in sacrificial, self-abandoned prayer.

Sacrifice and self-abandonment. There they are again. I take one of Betty Sweet's battered King James Bibles from my bookshelf. I see that she has underlined the words of Psalm 37, "Trust in the Lord, and do good; so shalt thou dwell in the land, and verily thou shalt be fed" (vv. 3-4 KJV). My grandmother's lengthy comments, scribbled out to the edge of the margin, are too tiny to read. *Verily thou shalt be fed.* I think of the delicious oatmeal she cooked for me, of the aromatic cinnamon applesauce that simmered in her kitchen even as she held this Bible in her hands.

Like Aiden, Betty lived a wholehearted way of faith, and she was surely a saint in her own right, a saint I could love. God-centered as she was, she somehow found a place for me too when her dedicated early morning devotional hours gave way to breakfast time. She calls me out of the lonely prayer closet and to her bountiful table; she gives God thanks for the food and invites me to enjoy the true blessedness of good things.

Mother Teresa 1910–1997

Stay Faithful [Anyway]

What you do, I cannot do.

What I do, you cannot do. But, together,

we can do something beautiful for God.

No saint was ever more in the public eye than Mother Teresa. Cameras followed her through the backstreets of Calcutta, trailed by her steadfast Missionaries of Charity. There she is on screen, giving her very life for the poor. As Mother Teresa bends down to embrace an HIV/AIDS sufferer, she declares, "Christ is in the poor we meet, Christ in the smile we give and the smile we receive." Her words are all Jesus, Jesus, Jesus. As the most sacrificial person imaginable, she drew from a bottomless well of warm, liquid, supernatural peace. Surely this woman who was named the "Saint of the Gutters" knew God intimately—and was completely known to God.

So it's a shock to read the letters published after Teresa died, for they recount an interior journey she confessed only to her closest spiritual confidants. Teresa's private letters reveal a woman who suffered deeply for decades, who felt abandoned by God. She writes, "In my soul I feel just that terrible pain of loss, of God not wanting me, of God not being God, of God not really existing." She laments that her prayers feel miserably dry and frozen. It gets so bad that she confesses, "I don't pray any longer." This revelation does not make sense.

Once the secret documents hit the press, critics like Christopher Hitchens decried Teresa as a fanatic, a fundamentalist, and a fraud. He declared that the world would be better off without her anyway; at last we'd be free of the consecration of her extreme dogmatism, blinkered faith, and the cult of a mediocre human personality. Although I certainly have no cause to dismiss Teresa as a hypocrite who didn't believe what she preached, I'm shaken by her state of dark faith.

How could it be possible that God fell silent for Teresa of all people—after everything she sacrificed in the name of Jesus? What could it mean that Teresa still proclaimed God's love when she herself felt spiritual darkness, even interior desolation? Her feelings of confusion, bafflement, and pain were no passing phase. "As far as we know," said her confessor, "Mother Teresa remained in that state of 'dark' faith and total surrender till her death." Now I am curious. Who was this woman—really? And even more, who was the Jesus she kept on loving?

Mother Teresa was born Agnes Gonxha Bojaxhiu, an Albanian girl who felt called to the religious life from a young age. We know that she was uncommonly brave, for she left home as teenager to become a missionary nun to India, truly a world away from Europe in the 1920s. Her adventure was off to a promising start.

As a novice sister, she fervently confided to a friend, "If you could know how happy I am, as Jesus' little spouse. No one, not even those who are enjoying some happiness which in the world seems perfect, could I envy, because I am enjoying complete happiness." She excitedly proclaimed herself the happiest nun in the world.

If you'd crossed paths with Agnes at the age of thirty-six, renamed Mother Teresa by then, you would've met a devoted but unremarkable teaching nun, beloved by her students at the Loreto Sisters girls' school in Calcutta. There would be no mention of the private vow she'd quietly made to God: she would refuse nothing of God, no matter what God asked of her. Teresa's pledge was to be tested in ways she couldn't have foreseen.

On September 10, 1946, an exhausted, overworked Teresa was sent for a brief retreat in the Himalayas. She was aboard the slow, grimy train to Darjeeling when Teresa plainly heard a voice saying: "Wouldst thou not help?" It was Jesus, she knew it. Clear as day, she heard him ask her to leave the safety of the convent and go to the most destitute slums, where Jesus waited in his most distressing disguise, the bodies of the poor. This happiest nun recalled her instant response, "The thought of eating, sleeping—living like Indians filled me with fear. I prayed long—I prayed so much . . . to ask Jesus to remove all this from me." Yet the request came again: *Wouldst thou refuse to do this for me?*

Teresa would always refer to this encounter as her "call within a call." She hadn't anticipated the immediate deep intimacy with God, the vivid presence of Christ. The voice insisted, "Come, come, carry Me into the holes of the poor. Come, be my light." Over months of conversations with the Voice, her new life of radical compassionate service took shape—and formed the iconic woman we know as Mother Teresa.

An obedient nun, Teresa was bound to seek permission to act on the divine message. The skeptical archbishop needed convincing; her request was unheard of, doomed to fail. Teresa proved relentless in her appeals, spurred on by the audible voice. When approval came at last, she wrote, "On Tuesday evening I am leaving the convent. . . . All is very dark—plenty of tears—Please pray.—I have very little courage—but I trust Him blindly, in spite of all feelings." Teresa exchanged her nun's habit for a simple cotton sari, and with five coins in her pocket, she left, alone, to seek Jesus in the desperate byways of Calcutta.

A few sisters joined Teresa as Missionaries of Charity to serve with Jesus, for Jesus, to Jesus. In the face of endless need, Teresa insisted on cheerfulness. To tend the suffering bodies of dying people was to touch the literal body of Jesus. Who wouldn't be happy, living intimately with Jesus twenty-four hours a day? Not everyone saw the appeal. One wealthy man observed Teresa cleaning the oozing wounds of an emaciated leper. Repulsed, he declared, "I wouldn't do that for a million dollars." "Neither would I," said Teresa. "But I would gladly do it for Christ."

Teresa always taught that God does not require success; God demands only faithfulness. Still, Teresa's venture was wildly successful. She labored nonstop, rigorous in her regulations, housekeeping standards, and daily worship. No, it wasn't easy—but, Teresa said, "In order to be a saint, you have to seriously want to be one." The Nobel Peace Prize, honorary doctorates, and donations piled up as the selfless Missionaries of Charity spread to 123 countries in Teresa's lifetime. When Teresa died in 1997 she was eighty-seven years old, committed as ever.

Teresa the celebrity saint never stopped speaking of the joy of serving. But unknown to the world, Teresa's companionable, guiding voice had gone silent. Jesus simply stopped speaking. It happened early in her ministry, leaving her alone for decades to grieve her loss. Teresa confided, "I am told God loves me—and yet the reality of darkness and coldness and emptiness is so great that nothing touches my soul." This is not an episode taken from inspirational Sunday school illustrations. It's not part of my spiritual superhero's tale. Why did Teresa keep smiling?

In making her private promise to God, young Teresa had done something perilous. She asked to share life fully with Jesus. Did she know what she was asking? In his life on earth, Jesus Christ had suffered on the cross. He had cried out, "Why have you forsaken me?" Was Teresa participating in Jesus' own suffering when she wrote, "I find no words to express the depths of the darkness"? With an unshakeable commitment I can't even comprehend, Teresa bravely converted her feelings of abandonment *by* God into an act of abandonment *to* God.

The worst poverty is not physical or material, Teresa often taught. The worst poverty is the distress of loneliness, of not being loved, of not being wanted. Anyone, whether they are wealthy or penniless, experiences the anguish of meaninglessness; these are the privations of our questioning, anxious modern age. Who suspected that Teresa felt that poverty too? She comprehended, in the depths of her own spiritual life, the pain of the poor left in the streets, "unwanted, unloved, uncared for, of having no one."

❧ ❧ ❧

Pain and loss are not part of the Christian life I was promised as a little kid in Vacation Bible School. Back then we all sang loudly together, "I've got the joy, joy, joy, joy! Down in my heart to stay!" And then we added hand gestures: "I'm so happy! So very happy! I've got the love of Jesus in my heart!!" I see now that our manic spiritual cheer was unsustainable. Yet I've always held to a vague belief that if only I got life with God just right, I would be blessed with calm and happiness. That loneliness would pass me by.

Some Christians say they "have peace" about a decision, peace being that happy feeling, evidence of God's approval. Teachers from other spiritual traditions offer techniques promising inner bliss. I know I'm not the only one going for serene assurance of God's presence and direction. Mother Teresa pushes against our expectations when she shifts the focus from feelings to fidelity. Turning the tables, she calls for commitment followed by faithfulness; affirming emotions are beside the point.

Teresa's story takes me back to our family record player, to the old vinyl albums of True-to-Life Missionary Stories for Children. There is brave David Livingstone, just off the steamer from Scotland, hacking through the African jungle to bring Jesus to what he deems the Dark Continent. He doesn't lay down his machete to ponder whether he has peace about the venture. Undeterred by man-eating lions, exotic fevers, and raving cannibals, Dr. Livingstone shouts, "Without Christ, not one step; with Him, anywhere!" It's been long decades since I envisioned doing the same.

Turns out I'm no David Livingstone and I'm no Mother Teresa. I do what I can. But extreme acts of mercy are just not for the likes of me, I tell myself. I don't feel *called* to it. Surrounded by stately white columns and prosperous neighbors, wretched poverty feels like an abstraction to me anyway. Yet every newspaper that lands in my driveway brings one staggering humanitarian crisis after another, day after day: desperate Syrian refugees flood Europe, young girls are trafficked for sex, homeless families freeze on America's streets. What can I do about all of that? I sure hope that inspired people like Teresa and her Sisters will step in, the heroines of compassion, to help. And soothe my guilt.

Will Mother Teresa let me off the hook here in my college town, a world away from miserable slums? I know the answer to that one. When Teresa met my sort on her worldwide travels, she'd say, "Find your own Calcutta!" God is close to you, God is with you, she insists. Watch and pray and you will always see Jesus. Look, here is Jesus, close by, present in every encounter, in each lonely undergrad or fearful friend. There is more than enough work to do, so just commit, the busy nun remarks. What you do, I cannot do, Teresa urges. What I do, you cannot do. But together we can do something beautiful for God.

"Keep smiling!" was Teresa's motto, and it always sounded trite to me. Knowing what I know now, I no longer dismiss her as an unearthly saint miraculously powered by endless supplies of divine rapture. She knew that warm feelings and bright words from God are unnecessary; faithfulness to Jesus is all. I hear in her words a call to courage: "We can do no great things, only small things with great love." Serve God even when emotion, peace, conviction fail. Put love into action. Stay faithful (anyway).

Brother Lawrence 1614–1691

Practice the Presence

One is not a saint all of a sudden.

FRIDAY MORNING FINDS ME IN THE KITCHEN, dicing four pounds of carrots and seasoning eighteen pounds of pork for the afternoon's Vintage lunch of barbecue. It's a Friday tradition at the Bonhoeffer House, a time to study the lives and words of older brothers and sisters in the faith, the people we like to call "vintage Christians." The college students who come each week yearn for their parents' cooking, I know, and the plate of homemade comfort is as good to them as the theological text we'll read together. Still, as I slide the ingredients into crock pots, a question comes to me unbidden: Why am I spending precious time laboring over food that will all be devoured in seven hours? Other people are running profitable companies right this moment, defending the accused in court, inventing cures for diseases. Cooking for a crowd is not so glamorous.

When I finally wipe down the smeared counters late this afternoon, after sixty students have come and gone, I'll have missed a day at my desk. In my world, value is measured by profit, by measurable outcomes; some might judge this meal a waste of energy and pork. They'd tell me to hang up the apron, order pizza and get on to more important things. The philosophy major in me deliberates the existential, even spiritual, meaning of my everyday tasks. I'm moved by a quiet, persistent sense that these mundane things are truly worth doing, that there is a gift here in the quotidian, something of value just for me. But what could it be?

❧ ❧ ❧

Standing at the sink, up to my elbows in suds, I think of Brother Lawrence, a man who scoured countless pots and pans back in his own day. Aside from our time spent in the kitchen, the two of us couldn't be more different. Brother Lawrence lived in seventeenth-century France during the brutal Thirty Years' War. This unlikely mentor of mine, born with the name Nicholas Herman, was a peasant so poor that he joined the military only for the meals and pocket money. The hapless guy was captured by the enemy, released, and then gravely injured in battle.

Once he was disabled by a chronic, painful limp, the young man was of no more use to the army. He managed to find work as a footman to a prominent banker, but the damaged, "great awkward fellow who broke everything" failed at that too. A brief stint as a religious hermit was another disaster. He'd expected solitude to be a safe, prayerful haven; it turned out to be like a soulful stormy sea.

Finally, at the age of fifty-five, the discouraged, agitated war veteran showed up at the Discalced Carmelite monastery in Paris. The Discalced ("without shoes") Carmelite Order was founded in Israel by some twelfth-century desert hermits who were deep into austere prayer and contemplation. This was a last resort; he'd willingly sacrifice whatever life he had left in him to God and the community. The Carmelites took him in. Without an education, their new recruit had no chance of becoming a monk, much less a priest, but he was admitted as a lay brother and given the new name Lawrence of the Resurrection.

Coming in with no background, barely literate, Brother Lawrence struggled to observe the Carmelites' rigorous spiritual exercises. Lawrence's first years at the monastery demanded theological study, penances, and services scheduled throughout the day and night. Brother Lawrence found that he couldn't pray according to a rule like the others did—he just didn't fit into this world of structured doctrine. He sat through mandatory meditation, but after it was over he had absolutely no idea what it had been about. His spirit was troubled and ashamed, for he dearly wanted to honor God. After all of his earlier failures, he wondered, was he a lost cause again?

To put Brother Lawrence's devotion and steadfastness to the test, the monastery's novice master assigned him to strenuous menial work. Undeterred, Lawrence declared, "I am in the hands of God," and did as he was told. In this way, humble Lawrence, the lowest ranking member of his small society, came to be known as the servant of the servants of God. Brother Lawrence confessed that, by nature, he had a serious aversion to doing kitchen work. But love it or hate it, he'd been assigned to scullery duty, so there he toiled among the scalding pots and greasy pans, day in and day out.

Brother Lawrence still wrestled, insecure in his own performances of piety. Then he had a breakthrough. He could simply do no more than love God—so why compare himself to the other monks? With that, Lawrence made a decision. "I resolved to give my all for God's all," he said. "I renounced, for the love of God, everything that was not God, and I began to live as if there was none but God and me in the world." The kitchen servant began a bold spiritual experiment, a method he called the practice of the presence of God. His goal was to be mindful of God's gracious presence in every day, in every single moment, in every thought—and to do everything, however mundane, for God's sake.

Now Lawrence encountered God far from the enforced reverence of the hushed chapel. For him the action was down in a sweltering kitchen where people rushed through, guests clamored to be served, dirty platters piled up. Even amidst the chaos, Lawrence had the only qualifications he needed for his spiritual project. It's not necessary to be super smart or have great expertise to go to God, he realized. All you need is a heart simply determined to adore God.

Brother Lawrence practiced a focused awareness of God right where he was. He behaved very simply with God and spoke frankly to God, asking God for help along the way. God was no abstract object of reverence but a palpable, constant, and supporting, personal presence. Year after year, Brother Lawrence turned his soul toward God. He grew into this practice of mindfulness, an inner habit of conversing continually with God in all that he did, down to the smallest action, to the point where, he said, "It is enough for me to pick up but a straw from the ground for the love of God."

Lawrence spent all of his days as the servant of the servants; the entire community depended on him. If a job needed doing, he'd do it. At times the monks sent him out on monastery errands, which was tough going with the crippled leg. Frankly, Lawrence never did come to enjoy kitchen work or limping through the crowded Paris streets. But, he said, "We must make our faith alive and by faith rise above our feelings." Feeding monks in the refectory or kneeling before the crucifix, it was all the same to him. His conversation with God continued.

Brother Lawrence's deep inner soul-life didn't make him unsociable. Those close to him described him as a warm person who inspired confidence, a friend to whom people could disclose anything. Underneath his coarse exterior, the kind brother always spoke with common sense and "a singular wisdom." After many years, when Brother Lawrence became too old and infirm for the galley, he was enlisted to make sandals. Finally he could sit down!

Lawrence urged others to practice the presence of God. As he counseled them he said, God is already an ever-present companion; simply cultivate that inward friendship. You'd think it rude to leave a visiting friend to herself. Why abandon the God who has come to be with you? Welcome God into your thoughts, even at your meals and when you are in company. It doesn't take much; your smallest remembrance will always be acceptable to God. You need not cry very loud; God is closer than you know.

Brother Lawrence's spirituality is direct, uncluttered. He boils it down to two sentences: "Think often about God in the daytime, at night, in all your occupations, in your exercises, and even during your times of amusement. God is always near you and with you." Could that truly be enough?

❧ ❧ ❧

I feel for Lawrence, dropped into a cloister of meticulous spiritual overachievers. I freely admit that I'm not like the Christians who get up before dawn to read their Bibles for an hour. I'm sure they never miss a morning. Yes, my devotional iPhone app alerts me to pray five times a day, but it's oh so easy to ignore the reminder chime when I'm in the middle of something pressing. Spiritual disciplines? Of course, I'm all for those! I head up a ministry. I'm a *professional* Christian, for heaven's sake. So why can't I get with the program like other people do? Just now I sense the truth in that popular saying: comparison is the thief of joy.

Newly inspired, I make a fresh resolution to continually practice the presence of God. But less than one day in, it's clear that I can't match Brother Lawrence. Nonetheless, scientists would tell me to remain optimistic. Research shows that it'll take me sixty-six days of repetition to establish an unaccustomed habit. (I know, I thought it was twenty-one days too. That's wrong.) If I can hang in there, it'll be well worth it; there are significant health benefits to prayer and meditation, the practices that will literally reshape my brain. Straightforward persistence is what I need.

Lawrence took years to form his habit, so the guy knows what he's talking about. He kindly reassures me, "One is not a saint all of a sudden." He is honest enough to talk about his past failures, when "a crowd of unruly thoughts would violently shove out his thoughts of

God." Lawrence learned to confess and then return his thoughts to God, gently calling them as if they were wayward children.

Lawrence admits that practicing the presence of God is tough in the beginning, but when it's done faithfully, it secretly works marvelous effects on the soul. Over time, God's love transformed him from a frustrated, discouraged outsider into a wise, free man. With the passing moments and days and decades, "his perseverance was rewarded with a continual remembrance of God," his biographer says. Brother Lawrence arrived at the incredible place where he could even say, "I no longer believe; I see and experience."

Back in my own kitchen, sweet, spicy sauce is simmering on the stove now. Text messages light up my phone while I shred the pork, hands too deep in barbecue to respond. I have some time to think about that old servant to the servants. Everyone around Lawrence had told him he was a loser. He was no kind of soldier. He was a clumsy footman. He couldn't even make it as a hermit. He persuaded the Carmelites to give him room and board, even though he seemed too dumb to learn the liturgy. Then God slowly turned Lawrence's world upside down. That beaten down man realized that no public recognition, no regimen of study, discipline, or self-denial would ever take the place of a constant conversation with God. The realization transformed his life.

What about me? I'm educated, gifted, and even coordinated. Why take out the trash, wrestle with the budget, or drive a child to the dentist's office? Isn't my time worth more than these everyday tasks? Brother Lawrence nods at the sign over my kitchen sink, the one that reads "Divine service conducted here three times a day." Then he reminds me that the gifts of this day are not measured in terms of greatness. Work, whether mundane or exciting, simply must be done—but God's presence, that is a marvelous grace in itself. God is present, close, loving. It remains for me only to pay attention again and again and again.

PART 2

Walking

Stand at the crossroads and look;
ask for the ancient paths,
ask where the good way is, and walk in it,
and you will find rest for your souls.

Jeremiah 6:16

THOMAS MERTON 1915–1968

Be a Real Christian

The gate of heaven is everywhere.

IT'S AN ALL-OUT FRENZY AS THE little kids in town converge tonight. The Lawn, our university's grassy quad lined by fifty-four student rooms, is the epicenter of trick-or-treating. Undergrads stand in doorways and drop candy into outstretched hands as the Halloween hordes file past. Where there's a crowd gathered, a Lawn preacher sees his opportunity to save lost souls. Evangelists are a familiar sight in this public space—and many are convinced that they've come to the very den of iniquity.

The Lawn preacher launches into a sermon on the evils of secular education. Shouting at the top of his lungs, his deep voice carries across the green expanse: "Repent and believe!" Burn your Satanic textbooks, he intones, and pick up a Bible; the Word of God is all that's needed. His hand-painted sign condemns our pagan institution, along with its wicked faculty and misguided students. Many of the undergrads passing by ignore the ruckus. Some shake their heads. A few mutter dismissively or laugh loudly at the preacher's dark warnings. Costumed children rush past him, focused on Kit Kats and Sour Patch Kids, as their wary parents shepherd them around the red-faced stranger.

Some may credit the Lawn preacher with bravery and conviction, as if he's seen the blinding light of truth and will bring it to us no matter what. He wants a confrontation today, but he sure won't get it from me. I look down at the ground, ashamed of the man's strident Christianity, his religion of threats and fear. I want to get as far away from him as possible. I'm keen to dodge any accusation that I might be one of those intolerant Christians. This has nothing to do with me.

In a world of diverse faiths, creeds, and cultures, the Lawn preacher perpetuates the stereotype of a certain Christian who's judgmental, hypocritical, anti-intellectual—a white conservative who refuses to accept the claims of science. As I avoid the evangelist's gaze, I think of another man, Thomas Merton, who was a Christian of an entirely different sort. If Tom strolled past us in his Trappist monk's garb right now, I'm convinced that the Lawn preacher would call him out as a heretic bound straight for hell.

Even so, Tom had countless admirers. Throughout the 1950s and '60s he was a best-selling author, peacemaker, and contemplative. The Dalai Lama, spiritual leader of Tibetan Buddhism, couldn't stop talking about his "brother" Tom—his luminous inner life, his true humility and deep faith. When the men met, the Dalai Lama said it was the first time he'd ever been struck by a "powerful feeling of spirituality in anyone who professed Christianity." The Dalai Lama would always say that it was Tom who first introduced him to the real meaning of the word *Christian*. Who was this Real Christian?

❧ ❧ ❧

Tom Merton was born in France during World War I, the son of peripatetic artists who raised him to be creative, a free thinker. His mother died when Tom was only six; ten years later, when his father also died, the grieving teenager was stranded at a stuffy English boarding school, where he refused to recite the Christian creeds in chapel, protesting, "I believe in nothing." Tom's freshman year at Cambridge University was a disaster of "beer, bewilderment and sorrow." Disgraced by his failures, he left England for the United States and enrolled at Columbia University, where he immersed himself in poetry, languages, parties, and politics.

All around him, the Great Depression wore on, and Tom continued to oppose God as a "noisy and dramatic and passionate character, a vague, jealous, hidden being." Yet within he was visited by memories of the beauty and quiet spiritual invitation of the churches he'd visited as a child in Europe. Tom became intrigued by thinkers like Etienne Gilson and Gerard Manley Hopkins, believers who wrote of God in Christ as *mercy within mercy within mercy*. Tom's heart began a slow turn toward this One who loved him and called out to him "from His own immense depths."

One drizzly autumn day, Tom was reading in his room on West 114th Street when something stirred insistently within him. Though he hardly knew what he was doing, Tom put down his book, threw on his raincoat, and walked the nine blocks to a Catholic church to tell the startled priest that he'd come to be baptized.

Tom never did anything in moderation. He journeyed far from New York City to Gethsemani, a Trappist monastery in rural Kentucky. Though it was Tom's intention to enter the community to "disappear into God," his superior, hearing Tom's story, urged him to write for the wider world. Tom's 1946 autobiography, *The Seven Storey Mountain*, was a surprise blockbuster book in which a well-educated, articulate young man chooses to withdraw from post-war society and goes to live as a Christian monk in an isolated cloister.

Tom's book brims with contagious enthusiasm. He rejects the American notion of happiness as defined by a profitable job, material comfort, and personal pleasure. Instead, Tom finds fulfillment and liberation within the constraints of religious life, bounded by voluntary poverty, penance, and prayer. Who would do such a thing? Readers were fascinated.

Some *Seven Storey Mountain* fans turned up at Gethsemani, inspired to follow their favorite author through the monastery gates. But there is no need to go to such extremes, Tom would say, for the experience of faith is for anyone anywhere. Wake up! he beckons us, and become aware of God's immediate presence through contemplative prayer. Though the word *contemplation* calls up notions of spiritual acrobatics "reserved for a small class of unnatural beings," Tom insists that it's a very natural way of prayer, available to each of us. Contemplation is nothing more than open attention to God at every moment.

The language of awakening to God is strange to my ears. It's so very distant from the lawn preacher's loud, fearsome, accusatory warnings. It's different, too, from the theology of my Reformed Protestant upbringing, the weighty vocabulary of total depravity, election, atonement, justification, sanctification. Could real Christianity be so straightforward? To listen for the joyful message: that God has chosen me and loved me from all eternity? Yes, Tom says, "this is so simple that there is no need to make a commotion about it."

In his telling, contemplative prayer fills the fragrant quiet of the woods. Back indoors, Tom writes, "Love sails me around the house. I walk two steps in the ground and four steps in the air. It is love. It is consolation." What a poetic way to live! Count me in.

Before I get too euphoric, Tom cautions me. There is a price to pay. Certain things must go: my distractions, my desire for things that pull me away from God, even my religiosity—those routine acts of piety that hold God off at a distance. There are no tricks or shortcuts in the spiritual life, he instructs, only humility and patience.

Alas, contemplative practice doesn't guarantee serenity, not even for the likes of Tom Merton. Everyday Gethsemani life was filled with irritations, usually in the form of other people. His solitude was interrupted by visitors and admirers; there was too little time to write. Letters and book deadlines kept on coming. He itched to leave for another monastery.

After much badgering, the abbot granted Tom a toolshed, an improvised hermitage in the forest. Even there, left all alone, he often felt tied up in knots. As it turned out, solitude would not be Tom's final destination; contemplative prayer was not to be a solo project after all. He was in for another surprise.

One day, a monastery errand took Tom to Louisville's shopping district. He tells the story of standing among strangers on the crowded city street and realizing, in that moment, that each person belonged to him somehow. It was like startling from a dream of separateness, Tom says, out of his own special world of renunciation and supposed holiness. In a flash, he knew the most commonplace truth: that the woman with the groceries, the Trappist monk, you, me, even Jesus—we are all together members of humanity. He looked and saw everyone shining like the sun. "There are no strangers!" he wanted to shout.

From that day, Tom pushed back against intolerance, the age-old self-righteousness of comfortable believers who judge everyone else to be automatically *wrong*. Rather, he insisted, Christ calls us to accept one another wholeheartedly, fully, and completely; it is then that we accept God. The protected boundary of Gethsemani dissolved as Tom perceived that "the gate of heaven is everywhere." Contemplative prayer turned him outward to engage with the needs of the world. Throughout the tumultuous 1960s, in letters, essays, and books written from within the confines of the monastery, Tom called American Christians to work "as brothers and as builders" of economic justice and peace.

Tom's prayerful openness took him far across the globe to Asia. It was 1968, and the Vietnam War dominated headlines as Tom traveled to a Christian conference in Thailand. While he was there, he met his Buddhist monastic counterparts and quizzed them about their experiences of the divine. The Christians and Buddhists, monks of different faiths, traded insider notes about hermit life: meditation methods, schedules, and encounters. They had lots to talk about. Tom and a Vietnamese Zen master hit it off right away. Tom marveled over Thich Nhat Hanh: "He is more my brother than many who are nearer to me in race and nationality, because he and I see things in exactly the same way."

Oh my goodness. I can just hear the protests. Naturally, our fiery Lawn evangelist would roundly denounce Tom for fraternizing with "pagans." Some of my Christian brothers and sisters would conclude that Tom bought into the New Age heresy that ultimately all religions are the same; sadly he's no orthodox Christian, they'd lament. In response, my nonreligious friends would be put off by the believers' condemnation, evaluation, division. Buddhism, Christianity, Hinduism, they'd say, it's all a mind game, so what's the big deal?

Some of Tom's own Christian colleagues fretted too. As Tom concluded his lecture at the Bangkok conference, no one imagined that his accidental death was only hours away. During the Q&A, a Catholic nun in the audience expressed annoyance. Tom had said absolutely nothing about converting people to Christianity, she complained. Why didn't Tom call on Buddhists to repent and be saved? In words that would be his last, Tom spoke from the heart: "What we are asked to do at present is not so much to speak of Christ as to let him live in us so that people may find him by feeling how he lives in us."

❧ ❧ ❧

What was it, then, about Thomas Merton that signaled Real Christian to the world's preeminent Real Buddhist? I wasn't there when they met, but I'm sure Tom Merton didn't come right out and tell the Dalai Lama to accept Jesus Christ as his personal Lord and Savior. Jesus was present between them just the same. From that day forward, the Buddhist said, "My attitude toward Christianity was much changed" by the Real Christian who was "a truly humble and deeply spiritual man."

Tom never lost sight of the risen Christ, the saving, living reality who stood at the center of his faith and infused all of his thinking. But because Tom didn't limit the everpresent God to his own framework, he could value the spiritual lives of other people, other traditions.

All this has me wondering how I might come to be known as a Real Christian to the people around me. I've rejected the Lawn preacher's unhinged fundamentalism; far be it from me to angrily divide the saved from the damned. On the other hand, I'm wary of a temptation to dismiss real religious differences between us, to avoid uncomfortable conversations by way of lazy tolerance. When I celebrate "diversity" as no more than a euphemism or a cliché, I miss precious opportunities to see other people for who they truly are, with particular commitments and complex convictions.

If I conclude that all faiths are alike in the end, then the notion of Real Christian doesn't mean much, does it? Yet God, loving and free, has every right to speak unpredictably. Ambrose, the fourth-century Christian bishop, once said that *all* that is true, by whomever it has been said, is from the Holy Spirit. Because the Christian life is a continual discovery of Christ in new places, I may encounter every person, whatever their religious tradition, with curiosity, love, and grace. And when I stumble in my own Christian practices, Tom's words reassure me: "We do not want to be beginners. But let us be convinced of the fact that we will never be anything else but beginners." I pray that I'll live in a beginner's attitude of open, contemplative prayer so that others may feel, somehow, the mystery of the Real Christ.

Benedict and Scholastica 480–547 and 480–543

Choose the Good Life

Is there anyone here who yearns for life and desires to see good days?

"Everything in moderation." What a dull cliché! Give me a thrill, a challenge, a climb. I've never attempted a marathon, but I do push my limits. Staying up late is a habit I perfected in school. Most nights I clocked three or four hours of sleep, propelled by wretched instant Suisse Mocha International Coffee. Exhaustion is a strange badge of honor, one I'm wearing to this day. When I cut sleep, I feed the illusion that my tasks are critical, that I'm indispensable. One more hour answering email just might buy me the compliment, "Wow, you're so busy, Karen. How ever do you do it?"

Tonight the alarm's set for 5:55 and a morning run with Erica. At best, I'll get six hours of sleep, assuming I don't wake up in the dark to rehearse the tasks I've neglected, the letters I really must write, the payment I forgot. Six hours. Any less and I won't make it through tomorrow without a throbbing headache.

I take short cuts. While I pack Nan's school lunch, I eat breakfast standing up, always the same coffee and toast plus a multivitamin. A protein bar at my desk keeps me going through lunch. Food and sleep are fuel I grab to go, commodities in short supply. My "efficiency" doesn't give me more hours off the clock; it buys me more time to feed my busyness addiction.

It's not my fault! It's the times I live in! Obviously, a sensible, rested life was easier to achieve in earlier eras, back when things shut down at sunset. What if I lived in, say, the fifth century? There would have been no electric lights, no 24/7 wireless connection, none of the clamorous deadlines and pressure I'm under today. Clocks weren't even invented yet. Seriously.

If I lived in the fifth century, I'd have all kinds of hours for uninterrupted prayer and meditation, out in the fields tending the sheep or planting potatoes. My family and I would sit around the fire, companionably telling tales and singing ballads. I'd be focused and serene, fully present in the moment (when not distracted by the occasional plague epidemic, itchy straw bedding, and a craving for steaming bubble baths).

Of course, the simpler times of the Middle Ages were anything but. The last Roman emperor was ousted by the invading warrior Odoacera in 476. Europe collapsed into chaos, a barbarian free-for-all of plundering by Vandals, Visigoths, and Ostrogoths. Under attack, the Christian church was ripped by conflict within. Glorious cities slid into decline, and the countryside offered little refuge.

About then, up in the Italian Umbrian mountains, the twins Benedict and Scholastica were born. Genteel Scholastica, like other girls of nobility, remained at home when her dutiful brother Benedict was packed off for Rome to receive his standard classical education. Once in Rome, young Benedict was appalled by what he saw.

Benedict complained that his privileged classmates were degenerates and that his rhetoric courses were irrelevant, each day a dull "cycle of studying and drunken partying." Why waste time at school while the whole civilized world was falling apart? Barbarians were literally at the gates. Benedict grew convinced that any hope for his society would require God's active intervention.

Disgusted by the excesses of his peers, the teenager considered his options. He had heard stories of earlier Christian desert fathers and mothers, those spiritual purists who'd opted out of Emperor Constantine's complacent Christianity and rejected the easy city life to live apart in the Egyptian wilderness. They were Christians who'd stop at nothing to sacrifice body, mind, and soul to God. Benedict esteemed their self-deprivation as one way to express both great love for Christ and detachment from the corruptions of power and pleasure.

Without telling his parents, a classic adolescent move, the boy slipped out of Rome and headed into the hills in search of a better way. What Benedict had in mind was a committed life of solitude and dedicated prayer. For several years, Benedict lived secretly as a hermit. Eventually, word of his devotion to God got out. One raggedy band of monks begged Benedict to come and be their leader and he agreed, reluctantly.

From the start, Benedict insisted on disciplined austerity within the community. But it seems that the monks didn't take well to Benedict's rigorous standards after all. In a bizarre act of mutiny, they poisoned Benedict's wine; his life was miraculously saved when the wine glass spontaneously shattered in his hand. Shaken, Benedict made a beeline straight back to the solace of his old hermit's cave, which he called "the place of my beloved solitude."

I imagine the arguments between Benedict and God then. Benedict claiming that he could do the most good there in his peaceful hideout. What could be better than praying for the world full time? God prodding him to get on back into faithful life with other Christians. Eventually, despite the toxic episode of the mutinous monks, Benedict ventured into community life once more.

When Benedict came out of seclusion around the year 530, he did it in a big way. He invited friends to join him up on Monte Cassino in "a school for the Lord's service," and he set up twelve monasteries of twelve monks each. His twin, Scholastica, left the family home to form a women's community of her own, just five miles away from her brother's.

From countryside and urban streets desolated by war and pillage, all kinds of followers joined Benedict: rich and poor, Romans and barbarians—even repentant Goths! Leading citizens of Rome sent their children over to Benedict and Scholastica to get them out of the dangerous capital city. Benedict accepted all applicants without respect to class or background, but he did require that newcomers commit wholeheartedly to two things: true love of God and unreserved obedience to the community's regimen.

Life in the monastery would be no freewheeling utopia, but Benedict wasn't about crazy sleep deprivation or extreme fasting either. Balance was the key. Benedict had the wisdom to see that the way we conduct our outward lives has everything to do with our inner spiritual health. The fact is, we need to be trained toward intentional habits that create space for God and for one another. When we're left free to indulge all of our personal preferences and quirky addictions, we are bound to suffer.

With that in mind, Benedict laid down some everyday monastic rules. Growth in holiness and harmony in life would develop through structure: a daily, rhythmic schedule of work, study, fellowship, rest, and prayer. Centuries later, we still have the details of the routine because they're outlined in his instructive text, *The Rule of Benedict*.

Benedict begins the Rule with a warm invitation: "Seeking his workers in a multitude of people, the Lord calls out and lifts his voice again: Is there anyone here who yearns for life and desires to see good days?" Look, God lovingly offers the gift of salvation, the way of true life. Why not accept, obey, and follow God together? With a unified purpose in mind, Benedict's code of conduct isn't meant to be about spiritual heroics; the rules are only there to promote spiritual health and communal peace. Humility and obedience are needed to help heal brokenness and safeguard love.

Benedict sketches out the routines of a balanced common life. He tells the monks what they will do, day in and day out, sunrise to sunset, so that each hour is choreographed to serve God and one another. The community will gather to pray eight times throughout the night and day. They will read through Scripture according to a set plan. The schedule includes a siesta, daily physical labor, adequate food, and, yes, a regimen of a proper night's sleep. (There it is—everything in moderation!)

Now, Benedict is not writing for spiritual superstars. He knows he's supervising ordinary humans prone to oversleep and cut corners. Like an attentive parent, wise Benedict anticipates the smallest practical issues, even when it comes to sleeping arrangements. Some examples: Don't sleep with anything sharp in your pockets (so smart—you could roll over and poke yourself). A nightlight should be left on (comforting, don't you think?). Sleep in your clothes (makes it so much easier to get to prayers in the middle of the night).

All property belongs to the whole community, to be shared without complaining. Everyone is given two sets of identical clothes; anything more is unnecessary. Benedict wants to head off jealousy and resentment, so everyone does kitchen and laundry duty, no exceptions. Even dishwashing is worthy of respect: treat pots and pans just as carefully as the vessels at the sacred altar. Anticipating some disobedience, Benedict lays out procedures for discipline and restoration of wayward brothers.

There is true genius in the Rule, for the Benedictine monastic communities founded on those guidelines flourished. Benedict and Scholastica changed the face of Christianity forever. As the grim years of the Dark Ages wore on, their monasteries sheltered learning, orthodox faith, and even civilization itself behind their walls. Even today, fifteen hundred years later, monastic communities faithfully follow Benedict's rule of life.

For Scholastica and Benedict, Christianity is so much more than an abstract doctrinal system. It's a complete life. They followed Jesus wholly, with body, mind, and spirit. Living in their own frightening era of excess and imbalance, Benedict and his twin sister saw a good way to live: thoughtfully, peacefully, and in moderation. Community life held them in balance day by day, and formed them in love for God and one another.

❧ ❧ ❧

Those twins from fifth-century Italy exemplify work-life balance, that concept endlessly discussed in women's journals, business forums, and wellness blogs. Buffeted as I am by my whims and others' expectations, I work too much, play too little, and pray too seldom. Scholastica and Benedict point toward the good rhythms of God's creation, where days are ordered and busy but never frantic. And I sure would like to get some sleep.

From the vantage point of my overscheduled life, Scholastica's setup looks ideal—the fresh country air, friendly collaboration in the kitchen, healthy meals eaten while sitting down, restful interludes for angelic chanting. I am drawn to a place where every day follows its own logic, where the deadlines are not up to me. (In my initial fervor, I gloss over the part about eight prayer meetings every day, attendance mandatory.)

When I take the time to read the actual Rule of Benedict, I find that it goes on and on . . . and on. My early zeal wanes before I'm halfway through the Rule's seventy-three chapters, bogged down in the section on "The Number of Psalms to Sing at Each Hour." Won't the cyclical singing/praying/reading schedule get boring? Who would want to live with all these regulations, under someone else in charge? The Rule just might be for control freaks after all.

I feel my independent nature resisting, my busyness compulsion nagging at me, as I visualize a real-life Benedictine existence. To get out of another contemplative prayer hour, I know I'd sneak off to take care of something more pressing (overdue board reports, piles of laundry, an insightful Facebook post perhaps).

Joan Chittister, a Benedictine writing today, draws me back to the founders' larger intentions. She says, "All must be given its due, but only its due. There should be something of everything and not too much of anything." In other words, everything in moderation. That way of living that I find so difficult.

But I see the merit in what Chittister says. Christ intends for us to have a good life that lasts forever, where God is the center of our rhythms, where companionship, worship, and service take precedence over productivity and accomplishment. Benedict calls for a reorientation, so that "no one should look after himself, but each one should strive to serve the others in everything" with love and respect. A joyful existence with lots of time for God and one another. What could be better than that?

To examine my own habits in light of the life that lasts forever is unsettling, especially when I admit that my daily routines have something, perhaps everything, to do with my spiritual life. I grumble that I'm overwhelmed, so busy, but, honestly, I'm choosing the way I live. I skip reading Scripture when I'm running late. I work for ten hours straight. I rarely bring God into it.

Why don't I just change my ways? "It is difficult to examine ourselves." That's an understatement. Luke Timothy Johnson, a former Benedictine, tells it to me straight, pointing to my jammed schedule as evidence of my self-centeredness. Johnson challenges me to "break the cycle of incessant chatter." He says, "One strategy is to recover silence in our lives. Stop, sit down and shut up. This is simple and difficult." Stop, sit down, and shut up? Certainly I can do that.

In view of the Blue Ridge Mountains, the sisters of the Monastery of Our Lady of the Angels live together, worship together, and make amazing gouda cheese. I've set aside one autumn day for a silent retreat here, psyched for an intense encounter with God. As the nuns chant, I slip into the small chapel during morning prayer. I wander outside to read psalms, write in my journal. Five minutes in, I urgently need a snack. I walk to my car and check my email from my phone. I know, I know, that's cheating. The next round of chapel prayer lulls me into an unplanned nap in the sunshine. Hungry again. I'm irritated by my failure to focus, to achieve my self-imposed goals for this spiritual field trip.

Meanwhile, the Benedictine sisters quietly go about the same routines they will follow tomorrow and the day after. Down in the cheese barn, elderly Sister Barbara likens her menial task to prayer, "like a communion with the Lord and what is becoming cheese under my fingers." Did Sister Barbara ever feel as I do? Unmoored. When it's time (finally!) to drive home, I turn the radio way up and roll the windows down, letting in the cooling Virginia twilight breeze.

Even though that little crash course in Benedictine spirituality was a letdown, it revealed the power of my compulsion to stay busy, keep up the pace. To change my outward habits and reorient my spirit to God, I'll need more than good intentions; practice is the key. This is the wisdom of Benedict. To make a start, I resolve to go to bed at eleven(ish). I put a daily alarm on my phone, a reminder to pause for Scripture at nine o'clock. I opt for quiet over radio news on errands in the car. I'm starting with mini silences here, and my resolutions look distressingly small. Ah, well. God, help me to stop. Sit down. Shut up.

Fannie Lou Hamer 1917–1977

Stand Up, Sing Out!

Christianity is being concerned about your fellow man, not building a million-dollar church while people are starving right around the corner. Christ was a revolutionary person, out there where it was happening. That's what God is all about, and that's where I get my strength.

THE OVERSIZED ORANGE BANNER at the front of the store blazes, "Welcome to your new AT&T Community!" Is this meant to warm my heart? The phone company has locked me in for a two-year contract, so I'm a member of the AT&T community, like it or not. The academic community, gluten-free community, cat-lovers community, mountain-biking community, cancer-survivors community—there is no end of community. We seek out people like us. We join the club.

Why, I've even got community right here on University Circle. Tonight the neighbors' association will meet to discuss trash pickup and commiserate over loud student parties on the street. I've got friendly neighbors who lend sugar when the cupboard is bare, but I'm longing for something more: a lasting community where my soul will find a home.

I hear "community" invoked at church, where the word sparks hope in me. Together we pray from the heart, we pass the peace of Christ, clasping hands. Shared meals bring back the Sunday school picnics of my childhood; even without tuna casseroles and marshmallow Jell-O salad, the familiar sense of family-friendly chaos remains. But community is inefficient. It takes time. When I slip out the side door before the final hymn, already on to the next thing—well, that's my own loss. Will I slow down long enough to commit myself to authentic community? Is there anyone or anything out there to pull me from my private orbit? And if I do join myself to new brothers and sisters, what will I freely give up for them?

For you and me, "community" can be cliché, vague, self-serving, safe, and sentimental. But there was once a "beloved community" of compassion and justice in America. It challenged ordinary people to face extraordinary perils in the cause of civil rights. One of those ordinary people was an unknown sharecropper from the Mississippi Delta. First recognized only as "the lady who sings the hymns," she emerged as a bold, prophetic voice for freedom. She was Mrs. Fannie Lou Hamer, and before long even President Lyndon B. Johnson would know her name.

Fannie Lou was an unlikely national leader. At forty-four years old, she and her family were just barely surviving; news of the emerging civil rights movement hadn't reached the plantation where they lived. Then one August night in 1962, she heard a rousing sermon, an invitation to claim the power of the vote and overturn the oppressive social order.

Fannie Lou was "sick and tired of being sick and tired," and right then and there, she heard Jesus call her to work for civil rights. She didn't hesitate. When they asked for volunteers to go down to the courthouse, she raised her hand as high as she should get it. "I guess if I'd had any sense I'd a-been a little scared, but what was the point of being scared?" she thought. White people had been killing her a little bit at a time ever since she could remember.

Fannie Lou joined a beloved community that promised liberty and empowerment, friendship and song. But from that moment forward, it would bring sacrifice, suffering, and persecution too. The very next day, Fannie Lou and seventeen others tried to register to vote. By nightfall, Fannie Lou had been harassed by the police, fired from her job, kicked out of her sharecropper's house, and separated from her family.

She was homeless and jobless but determined. "I made up my mind I was grown, and I was tired," she said. "I wouldn't go back." Fannie Lou dedicated herself to the work of voter registration. For ten dollars a week, Mrs. Hamer recruited new voters out in the cotton fields by day, and she led mass meetings in African American churches by night. She organized, rallied, and traveled, urging her fellow citizens to seek long-deferred justice, no matter what the risk. And she sang. "Singing brings out the soul," she pronounced. Even tortured and locked up in the Winona town jail, Fannie Lou's voice rang out with songs of deliverance: *Paul and Silas bound in jail, let my people go.*

Fannie Lou had no doubt that Jesus himself demanded action in the struggle for civil rights. Pious words were simply not enough. It's easy to say, "Sure, I'm a Christian," and talk a big game, Fannie Lou declared, "but if you are not putting that claim to the test, where the rubber meets the road, then it's high time to stop talking about being a Christian." You can pray till you faint, but if you won't get up and do something, God is not gonna put it in your lap.

Organizational meetings went far beyond operation strategy and logistics. The beloved community was no mere political affinity group; it was a spiritual, emotional soul connection. For the people who'd step out into the night, risking their very lives for justice, Fannie Lou lent divine significance to their cause.

The 1964 Freedom Summer initiative brought college students to Mississippi, starry-eyed volunteers from all over the United States. I can almost see them leaving home with their backpacks, headed South to rescue poor, uneducated black people from stupid, evil rednecks. But when one group of student recruits arrived at a Freedom Summer orientation session, they found themselves at loose ends, anxious and tentative after all. As they stood around, a woman whose badge read "Mrs. Fannie Lou Hamer" began to sing out in a majestic voice. She pulled the strangers together with rousing freedom choruses, songs that would carry them through the sweltering months ahead. The newcomers would be sorely tested but bonded by a common purpose. Black and white together, they too joined the beloved community. Fannie Lou mothered, admonished, and educated them all.

The volunteers were sustained by inspiring songs, righteous rhetoric, and tactical action. But their united front was assaulted by increasingly violent racism, hatred that was permitted by the quiet inaction of many whites on the sidelines. The summer began with the abduction and murder of young civil rights workers James Chaney, Andrew Goodman, and Michael Schwerner. Was the old Jim Crow system going to stand after all?

Fannie Lou and her compatriots were determined to give voice to people excluded from the electoral process, so they formed the Mississippi Freedom Democratic Party. The group traveled all the way to Atlantic City to challenge the credibility of the official all-white Mississippi delegation to the 1964 National Convention of the Democratic Party. The Mississippi Freedom Democratic Party, a rag-tag but determined bunch, demanded to be seated as participants in the convention. Mrs. Fannie Lou Hamer, African American native of the Delta's Sunflower County, one of twenty children, the girl who was forced to leave school after sixth grade to work in the cotton fields—that same Fannie Lou took to the national stage for the cause of her community.

Though he arrogantly dismissed Fannie Lou as "that illiterate woman," Lyndon Johnson was fearful that the Freedom Party would disrupt his well-orchestrated bid for president. He saw to it that the Mississippi delegation was blocked, but not before Fannie Lou delivered an eloquent, televised account of oppression in the segregated South. In her speech, she told the vivid story of her own suffering and of her people's struggle for civil rights. She and her brothers and sisters had come all this way and they were fed up—but they would not be denied.

Fannie Lou spoke the truth boldly in words that still inspire today. "I question America," she said. "Is this America, the land of the free and the home of the brave, where we have to sleep with our telephones off of the hooks because our lives be threatened daily, because we want to live as decent human beings, in America?"

Go to YouTube and watch this speech. While you're there, listen to Fannie Lou sing "Go tell it on the mountain . . . to let my people go," and you just may be ready to raise your arm too. It's no wonder that a fellow civil rights activist, Annie Devine, said, "Why not follow somebody like that? Why not just reach out with one hand and say, just take me along?"

❧ ❧ ❧

Like those 1964 summer student volunteers, I've been drawn to the glow of heroism from time to time. When I was their age, I tutored Cambodian refugees who'd fled the brutal Khmer Rouge. I imagined that if I equipped them with basic English grammatical constructions and taught the vocabulary words for foreign phenomena like "escalator," "washing machine," and "subway," then I would fix them right up for a new life in Boston, far from the killing fields of war.

Twelve weeks of free English lessons are hardly a great gift to the world. Yet I see now that I was offering up what little I had, young and unexperienced as I was. My English language students, most of whom were adults at least twice my age, accepted my good intentions and offered kindness to me. They fed me sizzling spicy cilantro noodles and laughed when my face blazed with heat. They handed me their babies to hold. They invited me to dance in a circle with them, hands upraised, wrists bent—and I fell into the embrace of their warm fellowship for one brief moment.

In my settled life these days, I carry the grocery store's Very Important Customer card. My university community, such as it is, emerges from networking and event planning, introductions and appointments. I am able keep my own identity intact, safe with people who look like me and share my preferences. But easy connections are fleeting, for they're built on shifting, shallow alliances.

Fannie Lou calls me into a wholly different kind of community, where belonging means both risk and true companionship. Throughout Mississippi Freedom Summer, people entrusted their very lives to one another. When I think of the civil rights activists, the tight alliances formed by their common struggle, I wonder how I have missed out. When was the last time I was that close to someone?

Fannie Lou's vision of beloved community was formed around more than a political cause; it was founded upon a living relationship with Jesus. One pastor who knew her well told me that "Mrs. Hamer spoke of Jesus casually, confidently, and constantly." She showed us how to lead as Jesus led: she offered up her life for her brothers and sisters, for people of of all races and ages—and all of us. Fannie Lou taught us that true unity is bought at great price, and she was willing to pay it, even at enormous pain to herself. In the hard places she stepped up first, leading before she asked anyone else to make a sacrifice.

Fannie Lou always saw the fight for justice as a spiritual one. Her faith gave her the insight to say, "Christ was a revolutionary person, out there where it was happening. That's what God is all about, and that's where I get my strength." She prayed with assurance and an eye on the concrete things that needed to get done. She sang scriptural songs of encouragement, even in prison after a night of torture. When the Voting Rights Act of 1965 brought in far-reaching voting protections for all Americans, Fannie Lou and her band of agitators won the day.

* * *

About twenty years after Fannie Lou died of cancer, heart problems, and hypertension, Charles and I drove up into the Mississippi Delta. It was a scorching afternoon when we paid our respects to this heroine of American history. We passed through Belzoni, catfish capital of the world, and on into Ruleville, Mississippi (population 2,874). We stopped to ask some kids on bikes if they could point us to the place where Fannie Lou Hamer was buried. Mrs. Hamer? They hadn't ever heard of her.

After some searching, we found the memorial stone standing alone in the middle of an overgrown field; I'd expected to find it surrounded by companionable graves in a tended church cemetery. We pulled the weeds away from the granite to read the inscription, "I am sick and tired of being sick and tired." We felt grief that she had come to be alone like this, anger that her own hometown children didn't know her name, bewilderment that so much courage and generosity would add up to this inauspicious end. Fannie Lou tasted victory but, ultimately, far too little recognition.

Since Charles and I visited Ruleville, the post office has been named after Mrs. Hamer. There's a large bronze statue of her in the new Fannie Lou Hamer Memorial Garden. If she were standing there now, Fannie Lou would beckon the children catching lightning bugs in the grass to sing, "This little light of mine. I'm gonna let it shine!" Camille would be there, our UVA friend who, inspired by the stories of Freedom Summer, has recently moved to the Delta to start a school music program with Teach for America. She'd pull me in too, urging me to action with a rousing song. No doubt Fannie Lou Hamer would see plenty of work to do, a community of people for me to love and serve.

John Wesley 1703–1791

Quit the Holy Club

Love is the highest gift of God. All of our revelations
and gifts are little things compared to love.
There is nothing higher in religion.
If you are looking for anything else,
you are looking wide of the mark.

Among our church congregation, my mother, Margie, was known for her hospitality, vivacity, and stylish hats, ever the gracious preacher's wife. She was dedicated to Scripture study, domestic order, and keeping us five kids in line. For Margie, Sundays were no day of rest. First, she'd get us all out the door to Sunday school and then to the eleven o'clock worship service. With the opening measures of the organ prelude, you'd find us seated in the third pew, mother and children all in a row, as my father rose to the pulpit.

Most weeks we'd be back at five o'clock for youth group and evening church. We powered through, fueled by free Krispy Kreme doughnuts, Cokes, and the fizz of adolescent dramas, all on offer in the fellowship hall. The routines of church were assumed in my family; who would think of opting out? As the upright oldest child, I knew what was expected: devotional fervor, steady demeanor, hair brushed.

Another preacher's kid, John Wesley, knew something about high expectations. His mother, Susanna, takes the prize as the spiritual superwoman of all time. Even with a large family to care for, Susanna never missed her daily holy disciplines or her weekly spiritual interviews with each of her children. Yet out of her nineteen kids, Susanna was convinced that little son John had a special call from God—and she intended to see him live up to it.

The pressure was on. Like other zealous Christian young men before and after him, John was ambitious in his faith. When an object of John's affection, the lovely Miss Sally Kirkham, gave him a copy of *Rules for Holy Living*, he went on a Christian perfection kick. He declared the "absolute impossibility of being half a Christian," and devoted himself one hundred percent to God. John regulated his life strictly, rose at four in the morning for prayer, declared idleness a sin, and rejected all leisure.

John was a true son of the faith. Responsible, intelligent, energetic. I'll bet Mama Susanna was mighty proud of her godly prodigy. I knew that my mother was gratified when I, president of the high school Christian Life Committee, left the house at dawn to lead a Bible study before class. She still talks about the night I brought thirty "unchurched" friends along to hear a visiting evangelist. The times I prayed with weeping classmates in a study carrel of the library. All that maternal soul tending was paying off.

Young John Wesley and his brother Charles left home for Oxford University. No rowdy frat parties or muddy rugby scrums for these two. Instead, the Wesley brothers, seeing "that they could not be saved without holiness," formed a spiritual society. Each society member was required to lead a holy life, receive the Eucharist once a week, pray, study Scripture three hours daily, and perform regular community service. These guys were hardcore, earning them the derision of other

Oxford students who mocked their "Holy Club" and called them "Methodists."

Energized by the achievements of the college Holy Club, John stepped up for the next sacred challenge: to evangelize America. He'd convert the rough colonists of Savannah to Christ and then move on to Native Americans in the wilds. It'd be awesome!

On John's trip across the Atlantic, an epic storm blew in. The sea broke over the ship, split the mainsails into pieces, and flooded the deck. "It was as if the great deep had already swallowed us up," John reported. "A terrible screaming began among the English." John was sure of imminent death and shrieked right along with the other petrified travelers. Then, through the driving rain, John saw something remarkable: a cluster of passengers calmly singing psalms through the tempest.

After the storm subsided, John sought out the people he'd seen at worship, a group of German Moravian Christians. John asked their leader, "Was you not afraid?" He answered, "I thank God, no." John pressed him, "But were not your women and children afraid?" "No," he mildly replied, "our women and children are not afraid to die." Then the German asked John a question of his own: "Do *you* have faith in Christ?"

Do you have faith in Christ? John's answer had always been an automatic *yes, of course!* Everybody knew that John had grown up with faith, lived for faith, worked for faith, talked endlessly about faith in Christ. He'd followed his parents' prescription for spiritual success. But what good was this confident faith if it deserted him in the face of death?

John's storm scare was the first of more tribulations; the missionary trip to Georgia was an utter fiasco. Unimpressed by the young minister's fancy title, Agent for the Society of the Propagation of the Gospel, the rowdy settlers rejected John's extreme Holy Club tactics. In a series of crazy events, John got tangled up in a romance gone bad, a hot church controversy, and a public trial, and then made a narrow escape from Savannah.

The upstanding young Christian evangelist had made a mess of things. He hadn't even ventured out of the port city to preach to the heathens. "I went to America to convert the Indians, but, oh, who will convert me?" John lamented. Whatever would he tell his mother?

How many upstanding church kids like me—the earnest religious ones who do everything right—sail boldly out into the world and are wrecked in the big waves? We hit rocky heartbreak or mental illness or career disappointment. We're unraveled by intellectual complexity or existential doubt. Our childish piety shatters like a ship's mast in a hurricane. John Wesley is one of us when he says, "I was indeed fighting continually, but not conquering. I fell and rose, and fell again."

John returned to England to regroup. Captivated by the memory of those unflappable, singing Germans, he got to know their Moravian leader in London, Peter Böhler. Peter spoke of God's tangible love, his own inward certainty of faith, and personal victory over sin in the here and now. One May evening in 1738, John stopped in at the Moravians' worship meeting on Aldersgate Street. There was no talk of spiritual bravado or rigid rules. The message John heard was simple and direct: *Believe and be saved*. Could it be? Was that all that was needed?

John's spiritual striving was undone—and that's when God acted most powerfully. The Holy Spirit brought about something dynamic, something alive: a fiery spirituality. That spring night, listening to the words of Scripture, John's soul woke up. "I felt my heart strangely warmed," he marveled, "I felt I did trust in Christ, Christ alone for salvation, and an assurance was given me that he had taken away my sins, even mine, and saved me."

John's encounter with God was no sugary magical moment or out-of-the-blue conversion. It was a personal reorientation to the biblical truths he'd already known intellectually. Now his faith in God was deeply his own. "Love is the highest gift" became John's new message.

Let go of that Try Hard religion with its expectation and image. Aim for love instead. "There is nothing higher in religion. If you are looking for anything else, you are looking wide of the mark."

John was resolved to preach freedom and grace everywhere. Freaked out by Wesley's enthusiasm, authorities of the staid British churches closed their doors to him. No matter: John took it to the streets, inspired by the example of George Whitefield, a pastor friend from Oxford days. "The whole world is my parish," John declared as he preached outdoors to impromptu congregations of up to twenty thousand people. Emboldened by a new pastoral calling, some days he preached four, even five, sermons.

John's listeners were working-class poor, people who'd been neglected by the established church and oppressed by the forces of industrializing England. They were seekers hungry for God's liberation. John talked about God's love, the essential heart of faith, as a love that goes out and gets involved in the messy world. John summed it up in a well-known aphorism: "Do all the good you can, by all the means you can, in all the ways you can, in all the places you can, at all the times you can, to all the people you can, as long as ever you can." Whether he was on the front lines fighting slavery or organizing his "Methodists" into small committed fellowships, John's passion was all-consuming.

Upstanding church people wished that John would bring Christianity indoors, back to the respectability of pulpit and pew, the familiar Holy Club disciplines of law, guilt, and doctrine. For John, once he'd felt his heart "strangely warmed" by the Spirit, there was no going back.

* * *

What about me? A childhood of mandatory church attendance equipped me to recite the major creeds, list all the books of the Bible in less than one minute, and hold my own in a theological debate. Even after I left for college, I remained diligent in daily devotions and

Sunday services—the outward practices that marked "true Christian" for me. I was still a church girl through and through, doing my duty, giving my assent.

Since then, years of shipwreck experiences (losses, fears, failures) have unsettled my spiritual self-assurance. I've handed over my shiny crown of piety, tired of being in church just to meet expectations. The ear-splitting organ postludes have faded. And that's a mercy. Now I feel that I've slipped out from the spotlight of center stage and down into a living faith where God is breathing spiritual life into my soul, and my soul is breathing love and prayer back to God. (Thanks for that, John Wesley.) Most Sunday mornings you'll still find me in worship, a few minutes late and sitting toward the back. I sing the hymns and say the prayers with a deep, even desperate, hope. I need, really need, God's wild abundant life—and a heart strangely warmed.

Francis and Clare of Assisi

1181/1182–1226 and 1194–1253

WWJD?

This is the advice that the Lord has given us; go and do as you have heard; and blessed be the Lord Jesus Christ who has pointed out to you the way of his angelic life.

I DO ADMIRE THE GRAND GESTURE. The New Year's resolution. The big, brash dream. But often, when it comes right down to it, I just don't follow through. Other things come up. I get tired! I make some adjustments, lower the bar, and settle for good enough. Is *satisfactory* so bad, after all?

Living in a place voted America's "Most Energetic" city, surrounded by top performers, I leave the competitive events to my gung-ho neighbors: rowing, hot yoga, mountain biking, rock climbing. There's a mini-triathlon for kids. I fancy myself an athlete but would rather skip the painful strength training and freezing predawn workouts. Out on a long run, I'm more than happy to slow the pace a bit. I am easily gratified, I guess. Or lazy?

I'd never be able to keep up with Francis of Assisi. He was intense—but he sure knew how to have a good time. As a boy, charming Francis

"Frenchy" Bernadone was a natural leader among the cool kids of Assisi. He was nicknamed "king of the youth" because he picked up the tab for his fraternity's late-night rambles. The narrow alleys of medieval Assisi echoed when he sang pop ballads in bad French. Francis's parents, Pietro and Pica, saw to it that he learned enough basic Latin, writing, and accounting to get him started in their thriving merchant business. Effervescent Francis was a young man headed for success.

Violence exploded when the town of Assisi declared battle against nearby Perugia, and bold Francis galloped out to fight alongside his good buddies from town. But Assisi went down in defeat, and Francis was captured. When he made it home after more than a year in a rat-infested prison, worn down by long illness and bizarre dreams, Francis was a changed young man. A war veteran. Childhood friends couldn't entice Francis to come out and party with them. What was wrong with Francis?

In agitation and despair, Francis turned to God. He took a pilgrimage to the holy city Rome, a walk of more than one hundred miles. He gave away his traveling money, traded clothes with a beggar, dressed in rags, and begged for alms himself. Strange. After Francis walked the hundred miles back, Pica and Pietro worried. The other young men of Assisi married and settled into careers or set off to join the Crusades but Francis wandered alone through forests and caves. If Francis were my son, I would have fretted too.

Rambling in the countryside one hot afternoon, Francis stepped into the chill of an abandoned chapel. In the stillness, he felt different inside. And then, it is said, from above the altar the image of Christ crucified spoke to him in a tender and kind voice, "Francis, rebuild my house, which, as you can see, is falling down." Francis glanced around and then, without a second thought, got right to work on repairs. He threw himself into the project. Francis moved from his parents' pleasant house to camp out at the little church near Assisi where he meditated, prayed, and worked.

In order to pay for the chapel renovations, Francis helped himself to valuable cloth from his father's shop and sold it off. To Francis, this wasn't theft. It was simply taking for God what was due to God. But that did it; Pietro was out of patience with his son. The story of Francis's public showdown with his father is well-known. There in the crowded piazza, Francis stripped naked and returned all of his father's clothes to him—in a pile at Pietro's feet—and declared God his only father. It sure seemed crazy, but in renouncing his privilege, Francis claimed the freedom to follow Jesus anywhere. He was done with the burdensome presumptions of his family, his friends, his suffocating town.

Out on his own, Francis was casting off his fear. Once he passed a leper by the side of the road. He kept his distance, looked away; from childhood he'd been revolted by lepers' oozing black boils and truncated limbs, terrified of their disfigurement. This time, though, Francis recalled Jesus' loving encounters with lepers. Moved by a sudden change of heart, Francis rushed back and wrapped his arms around the diseased man. In that moment of impulsive human mercy, Francis was shown mercy himself. Francis tasted a measure of healing within his own troubled spirit. He felt that he had touched Christ himself.

Francis found his one purpose. To him it seemed quite straightforward: he would imitate Christ in every literal way. Francis imagined walking along with a Jesus who'd time-traveled to the thirteenth-century Tuscan countryside. Every day, in each concrete action, Francis asked himself, "What would Jesus do here?" When he sensed an answer in the very moment, he would act on it. For real.

❧ ❧ ❧

In the 1990s, Christian kids took to wearing bracelets with the letters WWJD. That's right: What Would Jesus Do? In high school hallways or out on dates, the question was right there on their wrists, a prompt to think before acting, to "make good choices," as mothers often warn. I wonder if any American teen asked herself "WWJD?" and then did something truly daring.

What would Jesus do? Francis took Jesus' words seriously, literally, immediately. There they were on the pages of the Bible, clear as day. Jesus said three things that especially got to Francis. First: "Take nothing for the journey, neither bread nor money, and do not have a spare tunic" (Luke 9:3). Second: "Foxes have holes and the birds of the air have nests, but the Son of Man has nowhere to lay his head" (Matthew 8:20). Third: "Do not worry about tomorrow" (Matthew 6:34). Three sayings to shape a life.

Francis pursued what one critic called a "naive, almost manic imitation" of Jesus. "Do not have a spare tunic"? Francis, that cloth merchant's son, refused to buy clothes. He wore any old rough garment tied with rope; he gave up shoes altogether. Once the weather turned cold, he'd freely give away his cloak if he happened to have one. The Son of Man had nowhere of his own to sleep, so Francis slept under the stars or on the floor of a chapel. Francis labored with his hands in exchange for the day's meal, but he wouldn't touch money. He wouldn't even soak dried beans overnight—that was too much like worrying about tomorrow. Liberated from possessions and employment, Francis had plenty of time to care for lepers and collect stones for church repairs.

As he followed Christ through each day as a free man, Francis's old cheerful, generous temperament was restored. "What once appeared bitter to me became sweetness of the soul and body," he said. Life around Francis was weird but it was never boring. Folks were drawn again to his fun-loving manner. Before Francis knew it, others joined him, "brothers" who left their own privileged families to pursue the way of an exuberant Jesus. No doubt the parents of Assisi were outraged as their sons took off to live like that revolutionary Francis did, without property, without coins, without plans. Like Jesus.

In the piazzas and along country roads, the Franciscan brothers sang and danced, entertaining others as God's Jugglers. It was Francis, naturally, who got into the juggling idea. He named his merry band "Jongleurs de Dieu" after the medieval entertainers who wandered through town as minstrels and storytellers. In that spirit, Francis (who'd never sermonize in churches) would often preach in the sunshine, where he was known to dance, weep, play the zither, strip to his underwear, and even make animal sounds. His words were described as "soothing, burning, and penetrating." The citizens of Assisi couldn't help but listen.

Among the audience was a feisty teenaged girl named Clare. When she heard Francis speak of imitating Jesus she made up her mind to join the crew of brothers. Clare knew that there was no way her family would willingly let her go off and ruin her last chance for marriage, so at midnight Clare slipped away and ran to the Franciscans' forest campout. Before the sun rose, Francis sheared off Clare's long hair. This was a physical sign that she, too, would abandon wealth and position to follow Christ unreservedly. Too late, Clare's outraged uncles showed up at the Portiuncula woods to drag her home. The deed was already done.

Clare left it all to join the Jesus revolution, but her ambition to subsist in the wild with the guys was not to be. As a medieval woman on her own, Clare's only realistic option was to live as a nun. Clare's little sister Catherine and even her Aunt Pacifica entered her cloistered community, where they imitated Jesus together in their own way, praying, healing, and counseling.

Without intending to, the eccentric Francis had certainly started something. Men followed Francis in increasing numbers, women added to the "Poor Clare" sisterhood, all drawn to the Franciscan way of life that promised friendship, generosity, song, true piety, and simple optimism. You might say that together Francis and Clare expressed the fullness of Christ, each in a different way. Francis lived like Jesus in vigorous, earth-bound action. Clare imitated Jesus' habits of care and contemplation. Even in utter poverty, and perhaps because of it, their joy sweetened everything.

Pretty early on, the disciples of Francis got tired of juggling. The euphoria wore off. The unsettled roving band morphed into an established religious order. To commit for the long haul, sincere brothers felt that pragmatism was needed. They pushed for some lifestyle adjustments. They argued that sleeping in the rough every night is terrible on your back. They reasoned that the poor would be better served if they could collect money for supplies. They could still follow Jesus in spirit, right?

Francis would have none of it. Jesus hadn't changed at all—why ever would he? Going all the way takes grit, not compromise. Clare, too, held to her vows. She protected her sisters' spiritual health and defended their physical safety. When attacking soldiers threatened Assisi, Clare challenged them fearlessly, armed with nothing more than the bread of the Eucharist. Things got increasingly tense between Francis and his brothers. When the Franciscans were given a new house by a well-intentioned donor, Francis, in a frenzy, clambered up onto the roof, pried off the red clay tiles, and threw them to the ground. More "reasonable" brothers, exhausted by their founder's intractable standards, edged him out of leadership. Francis lost his own Franciscan community; only a few loyal followers supported him to the end. Even though he was heartbroken, disappointed, and ill after years of harsh living, he never gave up his zeal to live just like Jesus.

❧ ❧ ❧

I am all for the WWJD approach. As a follower of Jesus, it makes total sense. I mean, of course I *want* to imitate Jesus. I aim to forgive people who've offended me, to show love to others, to study Scripture, to pray. Jesus did all that, and I should too. But here's the thing. I'm about as extreme in my spirituality as I am in my exercise regime. I'm basically content with where I am, even though I know I could do better. I sit on the sidelines, cheering for Christians like Francis and Clare, the ones who go all out.

WWJD? Honestly, it's insanely tough to follow the literal call of Jesus, and failure is one hundred percent guaranteed. Francis and Clare of Assisi weren't perfect. They were sinners—two real, historical people—but they took to heart the challenge to imitate Christ. And then they lived with daring, even playfulness.

When I think of Saint Francis, I see him in concrete, a garden statue attended by precious bunnies and cuddly foxes, with a bluebird perched on his shoulder: a sweet, spaced-out version of the saint. The genuine article, that real hometown Assisi boy, was uncompromising and alive. *And what would Francis do?* I admire the sentiment behind Francis's antics and Clare's radical steadfastness, but they still can't convince me that imitating Jesus requires repurposed burlap tunics, never-ending camping, or a cloistered life. Nonetheless, I thank them for showing me the joy, the risk, the wholeness of taking Jesus at his word. Of trusting God for everything, careless and free.

That thirteenth-century juggler doesn't let me lounge on the bleachers, that's for sure. He urges me to get up and pursue the words of Jesus wherever they lead me, no matter how countercultural. With "soothing, burning, and penetrating" words he spins the dull preconceptions of God right out of me. Francis tips me off balance and makes me laugh. He teaches me a new game of faith, one that is both serious and utterly surprising. And he asks me to play.

DOROTHY DAY 1897–1980

Start Some Trouble

We are sowing the seeds of love, and we are not
living in the harvest time so that we can expect a crop.
We must love to the point of folly, and we are indeed fools,
as our Lord Himself was, who died for such a one as this.

HE STOOD AT THE CORNER of Falls Road and Cold Spring Lane every morning, holding that same battered cardboard sign: "Will Work For Food." With each passing day, my young sons became increasingly distressed; the man must be awfully hungry. Henry badgered, "Pick up that man! He can work with Daddy at the college!" "Yeah!" shouted Will, "That man can get paid to write his name—just like Daddy does!" Safely home, I packed up protein bars and water bottles and stashed them in the car, prepared to roll down my window and thrust a bag out to the man, just as the red light changed to green.

At age seven, sweet Nan marched out our front door lugging her jar of nickels and dimes, off to deliver it to a homeless woman she'd seen under a bridge nearby. When little kids see people in need, they respond naturally—often in fearless, personal ways. I'm less at ease in those face-to-face encounters with strangers, opting to volunteer a few hours or donate to a reputable nonprofit. So I offered Nan and her jar of coins a ride, and then drove her past the bridge and on to the Salvation Army where she skeptically surrendered her stash at the front desk. It's best to let the experts deliver care on our behalf. It's still generosity, isn't it?

Publicly, I am reputed to be a caring person. I cook lunch for hordes of students, host Bible studies and lectures, cheer on my husband and children. People unload their doubts, sorrows, and dreams in confidence because they find me unfailingly kind and sympathetic. But in reality, I'm shaky way up here on the superwoman pedestal. It's as if I'm teetering toward the edge when I hear a low voice in my ear whisper, "Do good, stay busy, but keep a safe distance." The sacrifices I make usually benefit people closest to me. Hardly heroic.

* * *

Nobody triggers a guilt trip quite like Dorothy Day.

As a little girl, Dorothy was drawn to the saints of her Catholic tradition, those noble people who ministered to the sick and suffering. But something really bothered her. Why this determined energy toward softening the effects of evil? Why not change the social systems that caused the suffering? Some saints ministered to slaves, but why not do away with slavery itself? she asked.

Well, if gentle, pious Christians weren't going to actually change the world, then Dorothy would do it without them. After college she threw herself into progressive politics, marched with pacifists and was arrested with suffragettes. She wrote for socialist newspapers. Among Marxists, pacifists, anarchists, and atheists in bohemian Greenwich Village, the activist life energized her. But after some time had passed, worn out by an affair with a married man, an abortion, and a failed marriage, Dorothy ended up out on a Staten Island beach, living in an unheated fisherman's shack with Forster Batterham, the man she loved. Forster was an honest, independent atheist who could never concede to the "empty form" of a legal marriage license. The couple wrote and worked and walked for miles each day, absorbing the brisk beauty of the world around them.

Dorothy felt the pull of the Spirit there; she wrote in her journal, "I am surprised that I am beginning to pray daily." But Forster was incensed by the very notion of religion, so Dorothy kept her prayers to herself. Out on the beach, Dorothy sang the "Te Deum," the ancient hymn of praise to God who fills the earth with glory. As she swept the cottage, she improvised devotions. She murmured the Lord's Prayer as she walked to the post office.

Marx's old phrase "Religion is the opiate of the people" interrupted Dorothy's thoughts, and yet praise of God came to her unbidden. She was praying out of simple, natural happiness. When she gave birth to a daughter she named Tamar, Dorothy's joy was complete. The final object of this love and gratitude, she knew, was God.

When I think of Dorothy Day the public crusader, I'm intimidated by her extreme acts of mercy. Here on the beach I meet a different woman, a young mother who walks along the water's edge, picking up shells to show her baby. This Dorothy is simply praying, praying with thanksgiving, praying with her eyes wide open to the sight of fishermen on the beach, to the sunset, the waves, the screaming, snowy gulls. I too have scooped up a child smelling of salt and felt pure gratitude. Perhaps I really have dismissed Dorothy too easily.

Dorothy knew that owning her spiritual transformation would cost her dearly, and indeed it did. When she had Tamar baptized and joined the church, the result was a searing split with her beloved partner. Dorothy agonized, worried that she'd become one of those Christian hypocrites. She wrote, "I felt I was betraying the class to which I belonged, the workers and the poor of the world, with whom Christ spent his life." Dorothy struggled to bring her newfound love for God together with her lifelong passion to transform society for the better. She longed for community. Then she encountered someone who would change her life.

Dorothy and Tamar had moved back to New York City, back to urban existence. There she met Peter Maurin, an older Frenchman in a tattered suit, pockets stuffed with books and papers. Peter was a vibrant Christian of an unfamiliar sort. He argued that the surest way to find God, to find the good, is through service to one's brothers and sisters. To love others is to love Christ, he said.

God brought Peter along to chart Dorothy's faith-filled purpose in the world. The city was crammed with desperate, unemployed people made homeless by the Great Depression. Where would they begin? Peter's plan was to start a newspaper and open up houses of hospitality and farming communes, relying on God to provide the funds. In their *Catholic Worker* penny newspapers, they wrote that Christ's self-sacrificing love made possible "a society where it is easier for people to be good."

Peter and Dorothy started the lay Catholic Worker Movement during a time of economic and human crisis, determined to live out Jesus' commandment to love their needy neighbors, quite literally, by sharing without imposing conditions or limits. Their gutsy personal charity was for real: they welcomed strangers, shared everything. The first Catholic Worker house of hospitality started a whole movement, sustained to this day, a Christian witness of nonviolence, voluntary poverty, prayer, and inclusion.

With her enduring passion for reform, Dorothy combined works of mercy and a daring brand of "political holiness." Direct action along the path of justice and peace was a way of serving Jesus, so she began each morning at worship in church and then hit the streets. Dorothy's unbounded generosity blew people away; they just didn't know how to reconcile her piety and politics.

When I picture Dorothy, I envision her sitting at a typewriter in a hand-me-down dress. I've seen her in black and white photographs: facing down a policeman, brandishing a sign of protest. Ladling soup into bowls as hungry men wait patiently. Coming out of jail, age seventy-five. Standing in front of a microphone addressing protesters. Serious, intent, determined. This is the Dorothy tracked by the FBI, condemned by President Herbert Hoover as a threat to national security. She's the public troublemaker who disturbs complacency.

The human, more colorful Dorothy comes through in her confessional writings. Yes, she admits, it really *is* raving lunacy to give up your own bed, food, and hospitality to any old stranger in need. But that needy person hasn't arrived to symbolically remind you of Christ. No, in "plain and simple and stupendous fact," your guest *is*, quite literally, Jesus. The Bible shows how ordinary people like Lazarus, Mary, and Martha welcomed Jesus and so can you; there's no excuse. Christ is all around you, meeting you in friends and outsiders. The glass of water you give to a beggar is given to him.

Dorothy insists that in the end we will be judged by our acts of mercy, so heaven hinges on the way we act toward Jesus in his frail, ordinary human form. As long as families still need bread, clothing, shelter, Dorothy says, "we must keep repeating these things. Eternal life begins now." So don't point to some distant dream of glowing redemption—let's make life *today* look more like heaven. Get out there and make a difference in Jesus' name.

❧ ❧ ❧

So what will I do? I can point toward the enormity of boundless human need. I may hide behind the excuse that my gestures are doomed to failure. I might even complain about the ingratitude I receive in exchange for the good that I do. Dorothy doesn't let me off the hook. She declares that my actions are measured by love, not by success. She assures me that God will repay me—eventually. If you love Jesus, then choosing to serve is simple. "Don't call me a saint!" she remarks. "I don't want to be dismissed that easily." She is unflappable.

Dorothy is also often quoted as saying, "The coat which hangs in your closet belongs to the poor." I know very well that at least one extra coat is hanging in my front hall. In her day, Dorothy shared not only her spare jacket but also her apartment, her food, her security, her energies—all without hesitation and in the name of Christ.

Living like Dorothy every day becomes complicated as the questions cascade. If I give my second coat to a poor person, what's next? If I load up the minivan with half of my stuff for the homeless shelter, will that be enough? Must I also donate my second car? My defenses go up as the boundaries come down. I imagine the eyes of Dorothy, gazing on me in disappointment. I hear her comment, "People never mean half of what they say. . . . It is best to disregard their talk and judge only their actions."

Still, I climb the stairs to the attic and cram five boxes with clothes I haven't worn in the last decade along with Henry's lacrosse pads and helmets, Will's baseball uniforms, and seven pairs of Nan's shoes, all at least four sizes too small. Driving away from Goodwill, I feel liberated from all that stuff, decluttered. But it's no sacrificial generosity—more like a token effort. I pull into my driveway and unlock the door. There, hanging on the hook in the front hall, are my coats: the brown jacket and the black wool overcoat, just back from the dry cleaner. I think of Dorothy, of course. Will I choose to give up one of them?

I'd rather fast forward, to the end of Dorothy's memoir, *The Long Loneliness*, the passage that always moves me to tears. She writes that heaven is a banquet and life is a banquet too, even if all that we have to share is a crust of bread. Hers is a vision of companionship, of evenings on the beach with friends and family, praying with eyes open to the glow of an eternal life that begins now. It's a beautiful image.

Living the vision every day is not easy. I don't just open up my hands to anyone who needs something of mine. I've never offered a bedroom to a complete a stranger, and I doubt that I ever will. I don't give cash to every person who asks. I've seen needs and let them go by without lifting a finger, even when I could have spoken up, stepped in, and tried to make a difference. Yes, I feel guilty about that. Because I am convinced with Dorothy that Christ is in every person I meet.

Jesus himself has told me that I can rely on God to provide for all of my needs. Dorothy constantly reminds me of this promise—and pushes me to act as if it's actually true. Dorothy both attracts and repels me, that loving, troublemaking follower of Jesus who lived what she believed. She's a saint who won't be easily dismissed.

Howard Thurman 1899–1981

Make a Swinging Door

Ultimately there is only one place of refuge on this planet for any man—that is in another man's heart.

I CAN SEE NOW WHY I GOT ON SHARON'S NERVES. The topic was racial reconciliation, so the organizers needed a person of color to participate in the roundtable discussion at our evangelical Christian college. Sitting next to me, I'm sure that Sharon was wondering why she'd ever agreed to be recruited. I was the zealous white girl, all good intentions, brimming with insights from my freshman Race and Ethnicity course. As the evening went on, Sharon's agitation grew; she was muttering under her breath as I chirped away. "What could *you* begin to know about racism, hunkered down out here in safe, Reagan-era suburbia?" she finally asked. "Come spend some time in my neighborhood and then maybe we can talk."

I was up for Sharon's challenge. The following Sunday morning I stepped out at the downtown Chicago train station where Sharon waited for me. We walked four blocks to her church and slipped into a front pew as the three-hour worship service began. I gave it my all, singing, clapping, praying, hugging everybody. At the fellowship picnic afterward I felt buoyant and welcomed until Sharon called me out. If I thought that a few gospel songs would remedy my racism, she snapped, I was even more clueless than she'd thought.

The two of us moved to a corner of the church garden, where we talked for an hour. Sharon accused me of ignorance, insensitivity, smugness, complicity. She railed against white privilege, capitalism, entitlement, systemic injustice, the segregated church, the mayor of Chicago—the crushing forces that made her life a misery. Most of her political references went over my head, but her emotion went right to my heart. Sharon was furious and I felt like *I* was to blame. I stammered. I stuttered. I cried. Why yell at me, of all people: the friendly college kid who gave up a Sunday to display her good intentions? Sharon had very good reasons to be affronted by my naiveté and to feel angry over the inequity around her. At the time, though, I walked away feeling only confused and distressed.

I wonder what Howard Thurman would have made of Sharon and me as we tried to talk to one another at that long-ago church picnic. Howard was the grandson of a slave and a child of scarcity. He was a man with no illusions about quick fixes. He knew very well that a can-do attitude is feeble preparation for resolving conflicts, especially those rooted in complex racial history.

Howard Thurman was a dreamer from the start. A child in Florida, he loved to walk alone on the beach, whipped by the wind of furious storms. "The very roots of my being were exposed by the raw energy of the sea," he recalled. Howard's everyday life was far less exhilarating. Segregated Daytona Beach promised nothing to a poor African American boy; his public school ended at seventh grade. But Howard's grandmother, Nancy Ambrose, insisted that Thurman excel in his education. When young Howard left home to attend a "Negro" high school one hundred miles away, his grandmother sent him off with the words, "Look up always; down never. Look forward always, backwards never. And remember, everything you get you have to work for."

Howard would travel as far as San Francisco, Boston, and even India—but his journey nearly ended before it began. Howard sat sobbing in the Daytona Beach railroad station. Bound for Jacksonville, the shy, brainy boy had spent his last five dollars on a train ticket only to learn that he'd need three more dollars to take his battered trunk. An elderly black man in denim overalls and a bandana took notice. "If you are trying to get out of this damn town to get an education, the least I can do is to help you," he said as he paid the bill and walked away. Decades later Thurman would dedicate his autobiography "to the stranger in the railroad station who restored my broken dream sixty-five years ago."

Because she could neither read nor write, Howard read the Bible to his grandmother. She refused to hear passages from the apostle Paul, the one who wrote, "Slaves, be obedient to them that art your masters" (Ephesians 6:5). Instead, Nancy Ambrose claimed the gospel as she'd heard it secretly preached on the plantation: "You are not slaves. You are not niggers. You're God's children!"

After he'd become renowned as a philosopher, preacher, and public leader, Howard would say that he'd learned more about "the genius of the religion of Jesus" from his grandmother than from all the men at Morehouse College, Columbia University, and Rochester Seminary, those professors who'd instructed him in Greek and the finer points of academic theology. It was Howard's grandmother who truly lived and moved from a center of deep, personal Christianity. She knew that social questions are bound up with the timeless issues of the spirit, that the search for universal truth begins with the seeker's own story. Howard often asked, "How can I believe that life has meaning if I do not believe that *my own life* has meaning?"

Howard would discover that meaning on a trip to India in 1935. At the time, India was still a British colony. As the white face of imperialism, Western missionaries were meeting resistance to the message of Christ. Perhaps black Americans, with their own history of oppression, would have more success? A leader of a "Pilgrimage of Friendship," the first delegation of African Americans to Southeast Asia, Howard was asked to speak widely in defense of Christianity.

After one lecture at the University of Colombo in Ceylon, a Hindu lawyer interrogated Howard, saying, "You have lived in a Christian nation in which you are segregated, lynched, and burned. You will pardon me, sir, I do not wish to seem rude or disrespectful." He paused and then went on, "I think that any black Christian is either a fool or a dupe." Howard answered that, yes, as a slave's grandson he was terribly sensitive to the churning abyss separating white from black. Yes, the traditional American church reinforced social and racial inequality. In fact, he himself was dead set against most of the institutional Christian religion he'd seen.

But, Howard insisted, the culture-dominated prejudices of "Christianity" are far different from the inclusive love of "the religion of Jesus." At its core, Howard told his challenger, the religion of Jesus is between a person and God, a relationship that is independent of abstract doctrine. A transformative encounter with God touches all of one's life—there is nothing that is not involved. The true religion of Jesus must take the side of freedom and justice for all people, for the "great disclosure" is this: at the heart of life there is a Heart.

The high point of Howard's trip was an early morning conversation with Mahatma Gandhi, a discussion that would alter the very political and social future of the United States. Gandhi, leader of Indian independence, was eager to know more about this religion of Jesus from his African American visitor. Over the course of their hours together, Gandhi examined Howard on the entire sweep of the black experience in American society, from voting rights and violence to discrimination and public school education.

Then it was Howard's turn to question Gandhi. "What do you think is the greatest handicap to Jesus Christ in India?" Howard asked. Gandhi replied without hesitation, "This is the greatest enemy that

Jesus has in my country—not Hinduism or Buddhism or the indigenous religions—but Christianity itself," practiced as the religion of colonialism. Both men, the Hindu and the African American, recognized the history of damage brought about by white Christians. What could be done to convey the liberating message of Jesus? Howard was captivated by his new friend's commitment to radical nonviolence, that creative, moral force rooted in the personal, spiritual development of love that holds the promise of genuine social change.

As their time together ran out, Mahatma Ghandi asked Howard to lead them in singing the spiritual "Were You There When They Crucified My Lord?" Into the silence that followed, Gandhi said, "Well, it may be through the Negroes that the unadulterated message of nonviolence will be delivered to the world."

Indeed, compelled by the nonviolent methods of India's struggle for independence, Howard returned to the United States dedicated to racial reconciliation. In a divided America, it looked like folly. "It was not only driving uphill," he remembers, "it was cutting the road out as we went without benefit of a map." In 1944, he left a secure academic job to establish the first racially integrated, multicultural congregation in America, the Church for the Fellowship of All Peoples, in San Francisco. Would Christian faith overcome society's imposed walls between believers? For a breathless moment in time it did, as a little group of diverse people embraced the dream of unity in Christ.

As a pastor and spiritual pioneer of the American civil rights movement, Howard insisted that we humans always have hope, even in the midst of the most barren circumstances. Why? Because God created us for unity and community. Beneath violence, fear, and power, there is an undeniable elemental human desire: to understand others and to be understood by others.

Howard never gave up on the "Jesus idea" of reconciliation, a racial healing that begins with individual spiritual transformation. Before nonviolence can take hold as an instrument of large-scale social change, he said, love must open the door of the heart so that what another is feeling and experiencing can find its way within each of us.

When he was called to be the dean of the chapel at Boston University, Howard's sermons found a national audience. He appeared weekly on the television program *We Believe* and was named one of *Life* magazine's twelve great preachers of the twentieth century. Among his listeners was a doctoral student named Martin Luther King Jr. "What is the word of the religion of Jesus to those who stand with their backs against the wall?" Howard asks in his book *Jesus and the Disinherited.* Howard's words would be a source of strength for King during the Montgomery bus boycott.

That same Jesus who lived as a poor man, who suffered under Roman tyranny, declares power for the disinherited today. Oppressed people can claim their own power by refraining from hate, Howard wrote. When people exercise their freedom to love, they demonstrate a strength that no enemy can ever take away. Howard's teachings on creative nonviolence came to be concrete political action. America was altered forever.

❧ ❧ ❧

By the time I came along years later, I knew very well that racism was a sin and that as a follower of Howard's same Jesus, I'd have to reckon with it. What would Dr. Thurman have said to me, that impulsive, guileless college girl? When another white person asked Howard's advice about what needed to be done in society, the pastor replied, "Don't ask yourself what the world needs. Ask yourself what makes you come alive, and go do that, because what the world needs is people who have come alive."

I do love the beautiful and poetic invitation to come alive. But whatever does it mean? And how could it have helped Sharon and me? Howard also said, "Ultimately there is only one place of refuge on this planet for any man—that is in another man's heart." To love is "to make of one's heart a swinging door." I must patiently find the openings through which my love can flow into the life of another—and through which the other's life can flow into me. A swinging door. More poetry.

Still, a lifetime of prayerful struggle persuaded Howard that meaningful, creative experiences between two individual people can be more compelling than the many ideas, faiths, fears, ideologies, and prejudices that divide them. A measure of understanding, however difficult, is possible.

Howard's advice turns to the specific. Peace between Sharon and me must begin with the discipline of religious experience: the submission of ourselves to God's work of forgiveness. Only God can pacify my inner warring parts, can heal and redeem and open the way for the discipline of reconciliation. And this reconciliation with Sharon? It requires three things.

First, she and I must deliberately *want* to be reconciled; only God enables us to want to repent of pride and love this mysterious other person. Without divine power, Howard says, we'll never even try.

Second, I must find channels through which my love can flow into her and her love can flow into me. We have got to understand one another somehow—and that takes imagination. To put oneself in another's place, Howard says, is the greatest adventure in all of our human relations. Imaginative empathy is nothing less than a miracle of God.

Third, there must be a sense of leisure in how she and I respond. We cannot be in a rush in matters of the heart. The human spirit has to be explored gently and with unhurried tenderness, Howard writes. It takes many agape meals and many long Sunday afternoons to learn this skill of tarrying. But if Sharon and I cultivate the discipline of reconciliation and give ourselves to wanting, imagining, and waiting for it, the rewards are great. "How indescribably wonderful and healing it is," Howard promises, "to encounter another human being who listens not only to our words, but manages, somehow, to listen to *us*."

Reconciliation is a buzzword among some Christians now, but how much progress have we made? In the society around us, racial hostility grows unabated as the enraged shouting grows louder, the grief deeper. I confess that I was not listening to Sharon that day long ago. In a rush to prove my innocence, my tolerance and Christian liberality, I saw the gap between the two of us, and I built a wall with my words and tears. Ready with her own assumptions and angry oratory, Sharon matched me, brick for brick. If Sharon and I had it to do all over again, perhaps we could linger for a while and try to find a way to one another. Instead of a wall, perhaps we could make a swinging door.

Julian of Norwich 1342–c. 1416

Rest in God's Goodness

Our Lord God showed me that a deed shall be done and He Himself shall do it; and it shall be honorable and marvelous and plenteous.

Optimism is that dogged allegiance to the glass half full, lemonade out of lemons, rose-tinted glasses. It's a stance that just doesn't fit today's world, where people everywhere are overwhelmed by violence, terror, and need. Even here in my seemingly safe little university town, dreadful things happen. Hannah has vanished, last seen partying at McGrady's Pub. At the vigil in the amphitheater, I look around and see the anguish on her classmates' faces, lit by candle flame. Fearful students, shaken, ask me to pray with them.

Tragically, weeks later, all hope is extinguished when the police find Hannah's body hidden in a ditch south of town. Back in the living room, huddled for prayer, we face the question: Where was God when Hannah surely cried out for divine rescue? My own teenage daughter, Nan, asks me, "Why does everything just keep getting worse and worse?" I hesitate, unsure how to respond, aware that this is no time to offer up cheery reassurances. Can I reckon with present darkness, dare I say *evil*, and yet—somehow, at the same time—rest in God's stronger, loving presence?

❧ ❧ ❧

I reach way, way back, 650 years into the fourteenth century, to find unexpected answers from a woman so enigmatic we don't even know her real name. Though she was the very first woman to write in vernacular English, we're not sure exactly when she was born or when she died. She's always been called by the name of the church where she lived—Saint Julian—in the English city of Norwich.

In her time, many people fully dedicated to the religious life withdrew into self-contained monastic communities. But Julian of Norwich was different. She was an anchoress: a common lay parishioner who chose to live alone in a simple cell built against the wall of her local church. Before the bishop, she vowed to remain forever in that place, a promise so inviolable that it was marked with a ritual burial service. Medieval anchorites, entombed with Christ, remained in their enclosures no matter what; even when attackers ransacked the towns around them, many burned in their cells. From our contemporary point of view, it seems like an odd way to live, but there was a certain brilliance to it.

As an anchoress, Julian could devote herself to prayer and contemplation and yet remain anchored to the everyday medieval society around her. Though she chose to live out her days within a small, walled chamber, Julian's enclosure was no undisturbed getaway. Her cell had three windows. The first opened into the church, through which she could hear worship services, receive Communion, and speak with the priest. A second window let in the sunlight and a view of her garden. Because the anchoress Julian was unable to provide for herself, she depended on townspeople and a maid named Alice for the domestic necessities of life. Julian kept a cat, the companion she described as "a certeyn creature that I lovid."

The third window of Julian's enclosure faced outward, onto the turbulent Norwich streets. Theologically, as neither a nun nor a layperson, and physically, sequestered between the hushed church and the vibrant commercial city, Julian was a woman on the margins yet fully engaged in both the church and the city. In her way, she established a safe space between sacred and secular society. Day after day, people walked up from the street to visit Julian at her open window, seeking her counseling and spiritual insight, telling her all of their tragedies and troubles.

Fourteenth-century England was a harrowing time. The sounds, sights and smells of death were everywhere. During Julian's life the Black Death swept through Norwich three different times, killing more than half of the people in the town. Those who escaped the disease were gripped by fear, sorrow, and the crushing labor of caring for the ill and dying. It seemed that the words of Genesis 7:21 would indeed be realized: "All flesh died that moved upon the earth." Some speculate that Julian entered her anchorhold after losing her own husband and children to the plague.

Visitors to Julian's window spoke to her of the day's terrifying events, darkly recounted as evidence of God's punishing wrath. Bad weather and sicknesses struck both livestock and crops, driving desperate peasants to revolt and loot churches and monasteries. From her cell, Julian got news of assassinations, the Hundred Years' War, stories of three men all claiming to be the true pope, of convents in moral collapse. Peering out onto the road, Julian of Norwich may have seen the condemned followers of the Protestant John Wycliffe go by, bound for a heretic's fiery death not half a mile away. It was a most unusual time to proclaim the boundless goodness and love of God, and yet this is what Julian did.

An incredibly strange thing had happened to Julian on the afternoon of May 13, 1373. She lay in bed, mortally ill. At the very moment she felt her failing body slip away toward death, she was caught up in a vision of Christ on the cross. During the next day, Julian, miraculously revived and awake, witnessed fifteen more "showings": vivid mystical visions that she recorded in *A Revelation of Love*. Julian narrates the startling revelations that appeared before her open eyes, visions of hot red blood streaming down from the thorny crown of Christ. She saw his dehydrated, crucified body and his bloodless, dry face. Jesus approached her as a nurturing Mother. God reached out as a beckoning King. Julian was visited by the one she called Our Lady Saint Mary.

Pick up *A Revelation of Love* and you too will see some puzzling images. In one "showing," God reveals a tiny object. It looks very much like a hazelnut and is as round as a ball. It could easily be held in the palm of your hand. "What is this?" Julian wonders. The answer comes to her: "This is everything that has been made. This is all of Creation." Such a small thing could easily dissolve into nothingness; how can it possibly hold together? Julian asks. Without words, the response arrives: "It lasts and it will always last because God loves it." The truth becomes clear. For God so loved the world. Everything—all of creation, right down to the tiniest kernel—is kept, sustained, alive by God's tender love.

In another vision, Julian sees her physical body as it is, clothed in fabric and covered by skin. In a kind of mystical x-ray, she sees further into layers of muscle, tissue, and bones, all the way to her sheltered heart. In her spirit she sees her essential self, soul and body, clad in the goodness of God, completely enclosed and safe. With Julian, we perceive a God who is no wrathful avenger but whose goodness is closer to us than our very bodies. There is an assurance that worldly terrors cannot touch us.

While monks wrote for other monks in their insular scholastic club, Julian of Norwich wrote in her local Middle English dialect. Her readers were the common folks she called "evencristen"—that is, her fellow Christians everywhere, of whom I am one. So when we ask, "Why does everything just keep getting worse and worse?" Julian hears us. Like the panic-stricken village neighbors who rush to Julian's window for guidance, I, too, worry about what novel, horrible thing will happen next.

Despite the immediate troubles of her day, Julian's mystical sights transcend current events; her writings make no mention of plague or politics. There's a way in which this omission makes perfect sense. In her revelations, Julian has seen the worst: God's innocent son tormented on the cross, a beloved child who dies abandoned and without an answer. What new thing could be more awful? Go ahead and bring your worst problem. There will be no sugarcoating at this anchoress's window.

In *A Revelation of Love*, Julian is a tough theologian puzzling over a paradox. Her visions suspend her between two intractable truths. She considers equally irresistible yet apparently opposing beliefs. On the one hand, sin exists: the world's appalling cruelties are caused by evil, and this real sin requires just and due divine punishment. On the other hand, God's love exists: the world is created and sustained by an absolute, absolutely invincible Love—that is, a God who does not condemn and will not harm. There is no harmonizing these conflicting truths. Julian is stuck with both sin and love. Love and sin.

Why has the powerful God allowed evil into the world? Julian admits this painful question. She won't soften sin with a fairy-tale ending, and that seems quite right. It would be cruel to write off suffering. So like you and me and the many of us distressed by evil, Julian turns to God and demands an explanation. She asks God, "Why?" The Lord tells her only that what is "unpossible to thee is not unpossible to me." This unpossible way will remain known only to God. In the meantime, Julian looks to Jesus' glorious resurrection beyond the savage cross, proof of the indefatigable goodness of God. She'll stand by the mystery: love's vulnerability is finally stronger than sin's power to kill. That is all she—and we—can know.

❧ ❧ ❧

"All shall be well, and all shall be well." Julian's phrase is often quoted in popular anthologies, written on coffee mugs and inscribed on plaques. In isolation, her words come across as harmlessly decorative, even naively optimistic. It sounds like the medieval version of "Life got you down? Don't worry; be happy!" A charmingly archaic Julian of Norwich, fluffy cat at her side, is reduced to the "pious periscopes" of blithe platitudes and glowing hazelnuts. This flippant version of Julian would never reach the hearts of distressed, sad, frightened ones—then or now.

The true Julian takes us on a bizarre journey through graphic "showings" gory with blood and leaking breastmilk. Julian points to the grisly cross as a sweet sign of Christ's friendliness, his courtesy. She asks to know the pains of Christ, to share his agony before his triumph, in a death that is somehow lavishly loving and joyful. This is very troubling business.

I am not as fearless as my sister Julian. I am never one to invite suffering on myself and, frankly, that would seem unhealthy. I back away from Christ's suffering, afraid and appalled. Like you, I long to get to the joyful ending, to resolve the dark mystery. I'd rather skip ahead to Julian's promise that all shall be well and that all manner of thing shall be well. Not so fast, says Julian.

She invites us to see the world with her, through all of its fearsome affliction, even young Hannah's murder or another mass shooting. In harrowing times, both then and now, Julian sparks hope. She tells us that the Lord will "give us more light and solace in heavenly joy by drawing our hearts from the sorrow and darkness we are in." We are held by a cruciform belief, there between the darkness of faith and the light of seeing. Because the love of God is eternal and overcoming, we need not be undone by the alarming events of the day. The larger story is the good story of God—but that story is not yet complete. And all will be well.

When the world floods me with anxiety, Julian of Norwich counsels me with confidence in God's good will. Why are you not fully at ease in heart and soul? Julian asks of me. I can almost hear her soothing voice speak: Little sister, you seek consolation in the things that are so weak, but in them you'll find no true relief. You are exhausted by evil and disillusioned by comforts that have failed you. My child, if you could only see that at this very moment God is nearer to you than your very skin. God's goodness enfolds you like a velvety blanket. God loves you and wants to be known, says Julian. Our Beloved is delighted when your spirit clings to him with all of your strength; so never lose your hold on his goodness. Let the God who is all-powerful, all-wise, all-good be your true rest.

Mary Paik Lee 1900–1995

Taste the Bittersweet

God must surely be leading us in the right direction.

If Mary Paik Lee overheard me griping about the lack of convenient parking, a weak wifi signal, or the ridiculously long line at Bodo's Bagels, I'm certain that the ninety-year-old woman would set me straight: "Life in America has changed so much that you don't understand the hardship we old-timers had to go through in this country." Young lady, she'd proclaim, this place is heaven compared to the place I knew in 1905.

She'd be off on a tale from her ordeals as a poor Korean immigrant in the American West, another time she was insulted, reviled, and excluded because of her race, tormented by her extreme poverty. Mary's vivid stories go on and on, all recorded in an autobiography she originally titled *Life Is Bittersweet*. How does an old woman recall so many details from her long century of life? "These things I've written down," Mary explains, "what I'm telling you now, I remember them because they made me *suffer so*."

Though Mary and I are both wives, mothers, and working women, our lived experiences could hardly be more different. Mary, born Kuang Sun Paik, had no inherited advantages to protect her from harm. I know very well that my race, education, wealth—dare I say it, my privilege—shield me from many everyday hardships. As much as I might find to complain about, the basics are secure. Yet Mary and I are both Christians. If we believe that God loves us both, why must one of us *suffer so*? And how is it that, in spite of the privations, Mary can speak out of gratitude, even contentment, at the end of her life?

"God must surely be leading us in the right direction." Mary's father and mother held this firm conviction from their early days in Korea, where the Paiks lived as a scholarly, prosperous family. Mary's father welcomed an American missionary and taught him the Korean language—the same man who, in turn, translated the Bible into Korean. By rendering the Bible into a very simple alphabetical system, Western missionaries appealed to Koreans excluded from the wealthier classes; Bibles were among the first written materials to be distributed among the common people, spreading both literacy and Christian belief. The Paiks joined the expanding ranks of new believers.

Christianity introduced transformative principles as well. Readers discovered unaccustomed notions of freedom in the Bible. Korean women, in particular, zealously embraced Christian teachings that challenged traditional Confucianism's bonds of female subjugation. Whereas respectable women had been forbidden outdoors during daylight hours, evangelistic "Bible women" traveled unimpeded to proselytize their faith. Leaders in the Korean independence movement, many educated in missionary schools, would be emboldened by Jesus' liberating words as they sought to break free from long Chinese and Japanese domination.

Mary's Christian parents and grandparents flourished as teachers, business owners, and ministers until the day invading Japanese military forces commandeered their home and forced them onto the street. Under threat of war and violence, Mary's parents hurriedly gathered their small children and set sail for Hawaii, where Mr. Paik was promised work on a sugar plantation. Looking back, Mary wrote with esteem, "Such strong quiet courage in ordinary people in the face of danger is really something to admire and remember always."

Courage would be required, great courage, for decades of interminable hardship were to come. Conditions in Hawaii were miserable: the family slept on the ground of a fruit plantation without a nickel to buy bananas. The Paiks moved on to California in 1906, a time when there were no more than seven thousand Korean immigrants in all of North America. Walking down the gangplank of the ship in San Francisco, Mary wrote, "We must have been a very queer-looking group." They were accosted by a gang of young white men who spit in their faces, kicked up Mrs. Paik's skirts, and shouted incomprehensible insults.

Why would we come to a place we were not wanted? the alarmed six-year-old girl asked her parents. Mary's father told her to remember the very first Christian missionaries to Korea, those strangers who'd traveled far across the sea only to be harshly persecuted as "white devils." As people of Christ in a new land, the Paiks would endure too, for God had led them there. They'd study hard and work hard and show Americans their true worth.

Even little Mary had to prove her strength. On her first day at Washington Irving School, Mary was surrounded by girls who hit her neck as they mocked her with a song, "Ching Chong, Chinaman, sitting on a wall. Along came a white man, and chopped his head off." Over the years, childish cruelty was matched by adult disdain, expressed in exclusionary laws and everyday offenses. Shut out of neighborhoods and public spaces ("For Whites Only!") and continually derided ("Dirty Jap!"), the Paiks struggled to simply stay alive. Legal codes barring Asians from most businesses codified the racism of fearful white Americans, citizens who didn't bother to see the differences between Chinese, Japanese, and Korean people who saw only nameless Asians, foreigners, outsiders. They certainly didn't care that the Paik family had suffered from Japanese aggression too.

Mr. and Mrs. Paik came to America with high hopes for a sustainable existence, though they knew that life in American would be tough. Mary writes that her parents "had put their faith in God and were determined to survive whatever hardships came their way." The Paiks labored without ever achieving the elusive American dream. Mary writes of the time that severe malnutrition caused her temporary blindness. The time her father ruined his health working in a toxic quicksilver mine. The time a rat attacked her as she slept. The growing family moved across California and Utah, chasing one grinding job after another. They worked in fields and orchards and mines until the pay ran out and they were penniless again. Mary would never complete high school. Hungry and struggling even to the end of their lives, Mary saw that faith in God remained her parents' only comfort and refuge.

As a child, Mary keenly felt the outrage of their situation. Later she would recall the year 1911. The Paiks had relocated again, this time to Northern California, but Mr. Paik still couldn't find decent employment because of what Mary mildly called "the negative feelings towards Orientals." In fact, the prejudice was so virulent that townspeople wouldn't even hire Mrs. Paik to wash their dirty laundry.

Without money, the Paiks subsisted on flour and salt. Mary recounts how, for months, her mother served them one tiny biscuit and a tin cup of water three times a day. Nonetheless, when the family sat down to eat, Mary's father always prayed, thanking God for all their blessings, something that never failed to irritate Mary. After one more starvation dinner, the child confronted her dad and asked how they could possibly be grateful. Mr. Paik responded with a question of his own, "Don't you remember why we came here?" The rest of their family back in Korea was suffering even more under the brutal Japanese occupation. They *would* thank God no matter the circumstance.

Mary names this as the moment when, for the first time, she saw beyond her own discomfort and awakened to "the realities of life" and the suffering of others. She drank water to fill her aching stomach, slept, and then got up to hunt for a house-cleaning job. Mary found work with a family who required her to come before school, after school, and then all day Saturday and Sunday—a job for which she was paid one dollar a week.

The young Korean girl trembled at the injustice of her situation. She was tormented by churchgoing Americans: white people who never knew that her family had taken pity on hapless American missionaries in Asia, taught them the Korean language, joined their Presbyterian church, and gone house to house to spread their gospel of love. As Mary spent another Sunday ironing from morning until nightfall, the eleven-year-old asked herself: where was their loving God now, in lonely California?

Not in the well-appointed Presbyterian sanctuary on Main Street, apparently. When a friendly high school classmate learned that Mary was Presbyterian too, she invited Mary to meet her at the church one Sunday morning. Mary's father, "always the optimist," gave her permission, saying, "Why not? Maybe times are changing." When they arrived early for the worship service, the four Paik children were blocked at the front steps by the minister who snarled, "I don't want dirty Japs in my church," and sent them away, shouting, "Go to hell!"

And yet the Paiks always found their own ways to create Christian community. Whether they lived in an improvised shack or an abandoned barn, on Sundays they invited other immigrant families to come over for a time of worship. Everyone sang hymns and prayed, Mr. Paik preached a short sermon, and then Mrs. Paik shared whatever meager food they had for lunch without ever passing around an offering plate. Somehow, together, they always had enough to share.

Mary would always remember her parents as the handsome, forward-looking couple who left Korea in 1905, confident that God would lead and provide, even in the face of evidence to the contrary. They held fast to the promise from Hebrews 11: "Now faith is the assurance of things hoped for, the conviction of things not seen." In her own time, Mary took up her family's strong faith and the risky hope that it demanded.

Mary believed that life was bittersweet—and she didn't let the sweet go by unnoticed. She married H. M. Lee, a Korean man who'd emigrated to Mexico. The two made a life together in California, planting rice and selling fruit. In their rental house, an old building with no bathroom and no hot water, Mary said, "I felt rich with so many things for the first time in my life," even a toothbrush and toothpaste. When the oldest of their three sons, Henry, attended Georgetown and earned his PhD, she saw it as the fulfillment of hope for things not seen. Mary's husband died in old age (with a big smile on his face, she notes) but he left her with a priceless legacy: "a feeling of great solace that makes life worth living."

For all of Mary's experiences of toxic anti-Asian prejudice, she lived long enough to see oppressive laws change and a new cultural landscape emerge. In 1990, at the end of her life, she was gratified to note that "Orientals are able to work almost everywhere now," demonstration of a patiently awaited miracle from heaven. Mary declared America to be the only place in the world where all people of all races can live in peace—so long as everyone obeys the laws and does their part to maintain harmony. She saw her personal sacrifices as "nothing spectacular but a good firm foundation . . . on which our future generations will find it easier to build their dreams." Hers are sunny claims I wouldn't presume to make.

❧ ❧ ❧

I've never been harassed for the color of my skin or bullied because of my native language. I've never been excluded from housing, rejected because of my financial status. I acknowledge that my whiteness and my family's economic standing give me advantages that I can't even measure. Even though blatant racism is a recognized evil and discrimination is against the law, ours is not a "post-racial" society.

Human hatred abides. People are sinful, broken. My country fails to live up to its promises of equality, success, amity.

But Mr. and Mrs. Paik followed God in trust and hope. Mary and H. M. Lee worked hard, studied hard, and honored Christ their whole lives long. And yet they *suffered so*.

Suffering. Mary couldn't avoid it. I don't expect it. The difference between us is so blatant I feel conspicuous, even ashamed, to be on the receiving end of unwarranted prosperity, benefits that I haven't earned. More than a few comfortable church people speak blithely of enjoying God's loving care, divine provision, protection, blessing, favor, while caring little for the material needs of brothers and sisters close at hand. Complacent Christians tell tales of sacrifice divinely rewarded, dreams come true, heroism, and happiness. But our plot lines come straight out of the American storybook, not the biblical narrative.

In what Mary calls "the realities of life," the righteous do suffer. She recounts her life story because she "wants young people to know the hardships that Asian immigrants have faced, so that they can appreciate their blessings today." Mary and her family didn't assume that God owed them a life of material security. They didn't interpret their suffering as a sign that God had failed them or that their faith was faulty. They just carried on, repeating that *God must surely be leading them in the right direction*. Out of their mouths, this is no soothing bromide, no entitled demand. It's a declaration of assurance in God's sufficient abundance.

From Job to the Psalms to Jesus on the cross, the cry rings out: "My God, my God, why have you forsaken me? Why are you so far from saving me, so far from the words of my groaning?" (Psalm 22:1 ESV). Like believers through the ages, I fight, I argue, I doubt. Why do some faithful people enjoy a wealth of good things while others struggle so hard? Why, God? Why the bitter with the sweet? I reach for trust, for confidence that God is leading and providing in ways I cannot see. That God is present, nonetheless, amidst my painful, unanswered questions.

Find Yourself a Soul Friend

Here we are, you and I, and I hope,
a third, Christ, is in our midst.

"We are constantly shedding our friends," notes an expert in the *Wall Street Journal.* From early adulthood on, our number of friends decreases steadily, though there are ways to reverse the tide. I skim to the end of the article, "The Science of Making Friends," for the helpful takeaway: five tips to starting a friendship. Ugh. Thirty-plus years out of college, the prospect of rejection chills my soul more than ever. I'll admit it. I'm prone to timidity, I still crave acceptance.

When I step into a circle of parents at a school function or chat up a new acquaintance at a professional conference, I'm alert to others' reactions. *What does she think of me?* the inner monitor asks. When the talk gets personal, I measure out revelations carefully, curating the image I project: put together, relaxed, friendly (but not overly so), self-deprecating, smart. In the meantime, I keep my true, unfiltered self under wraps, afraid to come out. True, deep, open friendship is rare—though more precious to me than ever. There's nothing better than a long, lazy dinner with someone I trust, a conversation when all the sensitive stuff is laid out on the table. But testing out a new friend remains a risky prospect. Would you love me if you truly knew me?

As I navigate the perilous terrain of relationships, I come upon advice from a surprising guide—Aelred, a twelfth-century monk who was nicknamed "Friendship's Child." From the pages of ancient parchment manuscripts, he recalls how he spent his whole life in search of friendship, saying, "Nothing seemed to me more sweet, nothing more agreeable, nothing more practical, than to love." Aelred knew both the human desire for trusting connection and the universal pain of betrayal.

❧ ❧ ❧

Aelred of Rievaulx was the noble son and grandson of Christian priests, born in a medieval Anglican kingdom that's now southeast Scotland. At fourteen, Aelred was adopted into the court of King David of Scotland as a permanent playdate for the king's sons. His warm, outgoing manner made him an instant favorite in the royal circle. He was promoted all the way to the top spot, master of the household, though he'd never been much interested in political power.

The schoolboy Aelred was obsessed with his pals. Like many youthful extroverts, Aelred flitted from one charming companion to another before mastering the basics of true friendship. He sought a deep bond but was often "deceived by its mere semblance." Even before Facebook, he quickly discovered that relationships are, well, complicated.

At eighteen, Aelred received an invitation. Some religious guys were setting up a Cistercian monastery following Saint Benedict's rules on manual labor, prayer, and community. Did Aelred want to join up? Somewhere deep inside, Aelred sensed the pull toward God. Still, the prospect of an ascetic godly regimen off in backwoods of Rievaulx, north Yorkshire didn't sound like much. He'd stick with the lively Scottish court, thanks.

Six years later, when an errand happened to bring him to the monastery, Aelred looked around and realized, to his surprise, that Rievaulx felt like his true home. He applied to be a monk the very next morning, ending his stellar courtly career. The change felt like God's calling, but Aelred knew he wasn't cut out for a solitary hermit's life. To his delight, he found that the Cistercian spiritual fellowship was a complex society all its own. Among the monks, this new arrival was reported to be "witty and eloquent, a pleasant companion, generous and discreet."

Aelred's integrity and natural intelligence, combined with long hours immersed in Scripture and prayer, formed him into a true spiritual leader. Before too long Aelred was elected abbot, and under his direction Rievaulx grew to more than six hundred monks. Years before, the monastic tradition's founder, Benedict, had called the monastery a school for God's service. Abbot Aelred envisioned the Christian community as a school of love. Aelred taught that the way of love—human and divine—brings vitality, joy, and fulfillment.

In Aelred's time, monks were forbidden to show partiality toward other individual brothers. I see some sense in that; people in closed societies tend toward competition and drama under the best circumstances. But in a break with tradition, Aelred encouraged particular spiritual friendships. Human friendships are praiseworthy, he said, when those relationships help us to love God more fully.

Now, Aelred had been around and he had few illusions about self-serving connections in the political circles and religious communities of his time—and ours. Like an experienced big brother who is wise in the ways of the human heart, Aelred gives warnings against two kinds of harmful relationships.

First, Aelred warns against "worldly" friendship, the kind of alliance that's about superficial benefits and financial gain. A worldly friend is always looking for the perks, the social networks you've got to offer. When you're no longer a valuable asset, you've seen the last of your worldly friend. Times are good till your credit card maxes out. Sound familiar? I think of the more benign relationships too, the ones born of convenience or common interest. They may be agreeable enough for a time, but when there's no substance, the friendships don't last.

Watch out for "carnal" friends, as well, who love you for your party potential. Carnal friends look for companions in crime ("to share mutual harmony in vice," as Aelred deftly puts it) and purely sensual, even sexual, relationships. If Aelred were here today, he'd see those people who want no more than a quick hookup or drinking buddy, throw up his hands, and say, "Such men love their friends as they love their cattle."

Worldly and carnal friendships will do you harm, so keep your eyes wide open to the motives of others, he advises. And what about your *own* motivations? Do you pursue relationships with some people only to advance your own selfish interests or soothe your guilty conscience? In a twist, Aelred reminds you and me that we are followers of Christ. This identity compels us to love everyone, even the enemies who are out to take advantage of us. Charity may hurt you, it may cost me, but Jesus has made his expectations crystal clear.

But wait! There's good news. Aelred holds out the promise of something far better than alliances that lead to broken hearts and sacrifice. That something is a *true* friend to whom you can fearlessly entrust your heart and all its secrets. Aelred describes a "spiritual friendship" that is rooted in the love of God—in which the foundation of faith is key.

Spiritual friends aren't looking to get ahead. Aelred describes this friend who weeps with you in anxiety, rejoices with you in prosperity, seeks with you in doubts. Nothing is faked; everything is in the open. A relationship that grows into something holy, voluntary, and true is one of life's greatest pleasures and a reward in itself. It's a "wondrous consolation" to have someone in whom your spirit can rest, to whom you can simply pour out your soul. Friends who stick close to one another in the spirit of Christ find that, along the way, they help one another to love God more deeply. So long as Christ is at the center, there's a partnership of three. Aelred writes, "Here we are, you and I, and I hope, a third, Christ, is in our midst."

Is finding a "spiritual friend" the relational equivalent of capturing a sparkly rainbow-colored unicorn? To his credit, Aelred concedes that this kind of holy, voluntary, and true bond is uncommon. He even makes the case that you can only find it with another follower of Christ. A treasured spiritual friend does not simply walk out of the forest. But all is not lost.

Abbott Aelred, the twelfth century's top relationship expert, has practical strategies to rival today's best self-help authors. He breaks the search for a friend into four steps: selection, probation, admission, cultivation. He even throws in advice on failed friendships. So here's Aelred's guide, "How to Find a True Spiritual Friend."

Step one: Selection. Not just anyone is right for your deepest friendship, Aelred says. Be picky from the start. Who shares your life, your values, your interests? Your Christian faith? Seek out someone who desires good things, who's discreet, patient, and loyal. I've known Bev for at least fourteen years. When we met, we discovered that we'd both gone to Christian colleges, have three children, are married to academics, and have backgrounds in education. It was easy to jump-start a connection. I've seen in Bev a grounded faith that makes space for my imperfections. She knows when to look the other way. She's okay when I say the wrong thing. She can set me straight, kindly. Bev shows up over and over again.

Step two: Probation. Take some time to test out your friend's true character before you fully commit. Is she truly there for you in rough times? Does he blurt out your sensitive secrets? I'm amused by Aelred's sneaky test. He recommends that you first disclose some confidence that, if betrayed, wouldn't mean the end of the world. Tell your friend something juicy and wait to see if it gets out. Aelred's version of "Trust but verify"?

Step three: Admission. So my soul sister Bev has proven to be patient, loyal, and trustworthy. Aelred says that once the test is complete, I should grant her my wholehearted friendship and never question her loyalty again. Always presume the very best. As Solomon said, "A friend loves at all times" (Proverbs 17:17). Spiritual friendship is for keeps.

Step four: Cultivation. Here's where Aelred's spiritual friendship reminds me of marriage. The commitment's there—and the relationship requires care and feeding, day in and day out. In the best version of our marriage, Charles and I anticipate the other's needs, lay bare our hearts, keep one another's secrets, love generously. Yes, friendship is the best medicine in life, but sometimes the tonic is difficult to swallow. When honesty calls for correction instead of comfort, we've got to conduct those hard conversations gently.

Abbot Aelred lived to the ancient age of fifty-seven. People were astounded! Though his health failed at last, Aelred was Friendship's Child to the end. Confined to the infirmary, Aelred welcomed groups of monks to visit him. One brother, Walter, remembers how he walked and lay about his abbot's bed and talked with him "as a little child prattles with its mother." Aelred was kind to Walter, saying, "Come now, dearest friend, reveal your heart and speak your mind. You have a friendly audience; say whatever you wish."

❧ ❧ ❧

Aelred's ideal was for single guys living a cloistered communal life, far back in the misty medieval past. Does it have any place in this secular, sexualized, commercialized, technology-driven world of mine? Friendship, like much of life, feels more complex than ever. We are more about healthy boundaries. In this moment I glimpse a span of one thousand years and feel the vast differences between a celibate Cistercian monk and me. God help us.

Aelred really has set the bar high here. I ask myself: have I even come close to experiencing this sort of trusting, authentic joy with anyone? I hold Aelred's silvery mirror up to my friendship with Bev or others whom I might call spiritual friends. I love them. I feel relaxed with them. But how far we are from Aelred's vision of "no division of minds, affections, wills, or judgments."

Does my husband, Charles, qualify as a spiritual friend? He and I fell in love young, got the marriage license, then made vows before God and a jammed sanctuary of friends and relations. We promised to share a family name, a bank account, a house, kids, and pretty much everything. Our intimate relationship is forever bounded by a very public commitment. Over our more than thirty years together, marriage has sometimes felt like Aelred's promised wondrous consolation—yet is often a maddening wrangle. We are pledged, but I certainly can't say that we are 100 percent united in everything. What would Aelred make of us?

I picture the private Aelred, apart from his role as spiritual leader, father, advisor of many. Did he ever find that spiritual friend he'd always wanted? He writes about one friend named Ivo with an intensity of emotion. He describes Ivo's devout countenance, charming eyes, and happy words. Aelred says, "Love increased between us, affection glowed warmer and charity was strengthened." Some argue that Aelred's writing on his "spiritual friendship" with Ivo is code for homosexual love. Yet despite the ardent words, Aelred's writings are clear on chastity, which remained for him a central monastic vow. Nonetheless, Aelred wanted no earthly gift more than the love of a friend, a soul connection, a spiritual ladder he could climb with Ivo so that the two could reach "the embrace of Christ himself." And a rare gift that is.

Aelred shakes me up. Am I content with convenient acquaintances? Can I admit to my own mixed motives and be savvy about the intentions of others? What kind of risks would I take for lasting spiritual friendship? Do I nurture the deep friendships I've already been given? And do my relationships reflect Aelred's compelling image of three persons in communion—my friend, me, and God? Aware of my need of kindness and grace, I venture that unspoken question once again: Would you love me if you really knew me? And I know that none but a true soul friend could unreservedly answer, "Yes!"

Get Practical

Our only desire and our one choice should be this:
I want and I choose what better leads to
God's deepening his life in me.

Decisions, decisions. I hear the questions over coffee in the Bonhoeffer House library. Apply to grad school or hunt for a job? Commit or break up? Boston or Atlanta? Take the higher salary with crazy hours or the lower paying job for a worthy cause?

Richard is nearly out of time. He's been offered a summer internship with a New York bank. His parents are pushing him to take it since it might lead to a solid job after graduation. But he just got an email from the orphanage in Nicaragua: Will he come down for three months to update their antiquated computer systems? He thinks of the little children he met there on the spring break service trip, how he'd left Nicaragua promising himself he'd find some way, however small, to make life better for them. And now here is the way, the concrete request.

So what will it be, investment bank or orphanage? Richard is struggling. If God has a plan for him, he can't see or feel it. With two more days to make a choice, he admits that he has opened up his Bible, praying that the page would fall open to a clue. Richard is casting around for a word, a dream, a sign, something clear.

I write effusive recommendation letters for students applying to internships, first jobs, nonprofits, graduate schools, the Peace Corps. I am strong on superlatives and emotional adjectives but I cannot answer that crucial question: "Is this the way to God's will?"

❧ ❧ ❧

When all of life is ahead, the view is of countless twisting paths and trails that lead off in all kinds of directions. Is God's will found in a divine game of hide and seek, a chase through some cosmic maze? Is it a puzzle with one single solution? What becomes of wrong turns and blind alleys? For the confused and perplexed, Ignatius of Loyola steps in like a rational older brother, ready with a strategy for sorting things out. Ignatius's organized approach to the spiritual life reveals his training as a military man. He writes out concrete lists and processes that contain real spiritual know-how.

Ignatius was one of those bold, confident guys. He was die-hard, all in, going for broke. An aristocrat from Loyola in the Basque region of northern Spain, Ignatius had it all, castle included. With money and handsome looks, he distinguished himself as a young page in a nobleman's court. The ladies loved the way he looked in fitted tights, gleaming armor and sky blue doublet, sparking rumors of an illegitimate child. And as a high-spirited, manly soldier, Ignatius had a police record for nighttime brawling with intent to inflict serious harm.

Writing his memoir years later, Ignatius recalls that he was a young man "given to the vanities of the world; and what he enjoyed most was warlike sport, with a great and foolish desire to win fame." When the French attacked the Spanish fortress at Pamplona and his fellow officers were ready to surrender, Ignatius would have none of their cowardice, choosing instead the path of doomed valor. "Bring it on!" he roared (in so many words), brandishing his saber. In the mayhem that followed, a cannonball ripped through Ignatius's leg and brought him down.

Ignatius, shattered and humiliated, was carried back to the family's drafty castle to recuperate. The damaged leg healed badly, ruining his profile in courtier's hose. He insisted on a series of agonizing operations, without the benefit of anesthesia, of course, but his leg was never the same. To make things worse, stuck in bed and longing for a tall stack of chivalric adventure romances to pass the time, Ignatius found that the only reading materials in the castle were dry devotional books, biographies of the saints, and stories about Jesus.

Bored, Ignatius browsed through the books at hand, and even there he discovered a challenge to fire his competitive nature. Reading narratives of Jesus and of the saints, Ignatius stopped to think, "Hey, what if I were to do what Saint Francis or Saint Dominic did?" Those fellows were champions in the religious arena, so Ignatius would beat them on their terms. He would do them one better in zeal, focus, and devotion to God. Ignatius believed that if Saint Dominic debated theology with heretics, he would do it too. If Saint Francis gave up his material wealth to live in complete poverty, then he would do the same.

Once his convalescence was complete, the newly converted Ignatius went extreme with the fasting, vigils, endless hours on his knees. Where he had once obsessed over trendy courtier style, now Ignatius refused to cut his hair and fingernails in a physical demonstration of his total repentance.

At first, Ignatius's holy resolution looked like another macho phase. But as he imagined a real future in God's service, Ignatius was filled with *consolation*—the name he gave to feeling on fire with God's love, vibrantly alive and connected to others. In contrast, thoughts of returning to the glories of the court or the battlefield left his soul in *desolation*, the feeling of being "without hope and without love."

Ignatius devoted himself to solitary prayer, and he came to know God in a deeper way. It was a novel sensation, this awareness of God's movement through consolation and desolation, an interior experience that helped Ignatius discern God's will for his life. No half degrees here, of course. In a grand flourish, he laid his sword and dagger on the altar of Our Lady in Monserrat, and his transformation into a soldier of Christ was complete.

Ignatius was, as you know by now, a man of action. So once fencing and gambling were out, prayer and preaching were in. He drew from his own intimate personal encounters with God to create a method, a prayer program for the rest of us. It's laid out in the *Spiritual Exercises*, Ignatius's how-to manual for spiritual retreat. Yes, you can pick up the book on Amazon, but don't expect to curl up with a volume of heart-warming tales or inspirational poetry. You'll find that the *Spiritual Exercises* are a handbook of life with God, a user's guide to the soul.

The *Spiritual Exercises* lay out a four-week plan. If you take up the challenge, here's what to expect. During the first week, you will confront your sin and admit to the bad choices that hold you back. In week two, you will prayerfully consider new directions for your life. The third week takes you on a deep dive into the life and example of Jesus. In week four, you will meditate on the promises of God to bring about your ultimate good through the power of the risen Christ. The series of rigorous spiritual workouts will move you out of the narrow, self-referential way you're living now and push you up and toward reliance on God's will for your life.

Ignatius had a gift for *practical* faith. If Ignatius were here to sit down with my friend Richard, he would lay out a "way of proceeding" through the young man's bank internship versus orphanage dilemma. Just as Ignatius came up with a four-week plan of spiritual exercises, he envisioned a method for making decisions. The abbreviated version of Ignatius's methodical discernment process looks something like this: begin with the central question, "What will bring the greatest glory to God?" This is the goal. Got it?

Then, to reach an answer, he'd say, follow the steps. First, identify the issue and clearly define the decision at hand. Second, pray for sincere openness to God's will, whatever that might be. But be honest; you may find that you have already made up your mind. If so, go back and repeat step two: pray for true openness and make sure you mean it this time!

You're not done yet, Ignatius says. Third, gather all the necessary information about the options in front of you. List pros and cons. Go ahead, write it all down. Fourth, ask God to give you clear thoughts and feelings. Be aware of consolation (that vibrant, alive feeling of connection to God and others) or desolation (an inward spiral of negative, draining sensations). Pray, pray, pray for God's guidance. Speak with a spiritual advisor. *Fifth* step? Boldly make that decision. Now go forward in freedom, confident in God's direction. Done.

Ignatius was passionate about this intensive Spiritual Exercises workout he'd developed, and he was eager to take it to the world. But even with his mastery of sword skills and courtly etiquette, he knew he'd need more education to move forward in ministry.

So at thirty years old, Ignatius started over with elementary Latin, sitting in class with schoolboys half his age. He kept at his studies until he made it to the University of Paris. By then he was trimming his fingernails again, thank goodness, but his enthusiasm for God still set him apart.

Ignatius coached his roommate, Francis Xavier, through the spiritual fitness regimen, and they mobilized four more college friends to join in their devotional routines. The Spiritual Exercises caught on; three of Ignatius's University of Paris professors even quit teaching to go full time on Team Ignatius.

There must have been a lot of talk in the faculty lounge about this radical group of guys who called themselves the Society of Jesus. Critics mocked them as "Jesuits." Jesus-ites. Jesus Freaks. It was the sixteenth century, after all, when people expected religious brothers to leave public life and join self-contained communities inside monastery walls. These enthusiastic Jesuits took Christianity in a new direction: dispatched by Ignatius, they headed out to teach and evangelize the world. Ignatius's companion, Peter Faber, witnessed all over

Europe. With only a breviary and a pair of boots, Francis Xavier trekked from India to Japan to China preaching the gospel. Within their founder's lifetime, a global missionary movement began.

❧ ❧ ❧

Even today, Jesuits live by the motto *ad majorem Dei gloriam*: "For the greater glory of God." I for one am drawn to the idea of the glory of God, absolutely. Even so, I'm intimidated by the historical Ignatius, the super zealous coach who was always recruiting, organizing, programming. The physical portrait of the man, with his piercing eyes, stern brow, and black robe, doesn't warm my heart much. I wouldn't have expected this Ignatius to bring grace and freedom to my own spiritual life. To my amazement, he has.

Here's what I mean. The Ten Commandments, the creeds of the church, the "red letter" teachings of Jesus, the words of reputable Christians—those spiritual authorities have always felt like solid ground to me. But guess what? Life is complex. So very many times, the tried and true principles of my Christian faith are short on specifics; I have no map to guide me through thorny questions and impossible decisions.

At those bewildering moments, older brother Ignatius assures me that I already have all I that need to live a confident spiritual life. Ignatius trusts me to discern God's purposes here in my own particular culture, history, and personality. Or rather, Ignatius trusts *God* to reach me in my own here and now. If only I will slow down and listen for God's voice, God will make the way clear. Or, at least, clear enough to illuminate the next step.

The Spiritual Exercises return me to the basics. Ignatius begins, "The goal of our life is to live with God forever. God, who loves us, gave us life. Our own response of love allows God's life to flow into us without limit." Already, Ignatius helps me relax my grip on religious rules and open my heart to the dynamics of God's love.

So much talk about life, about *love*. I can release my need to do things right, follow narrow rules, or anxiously appeal to established authority. It all comes down to one thing, Ignatius says: "Our only desire and our one choice should be this: I want and I choose what better leads to God's deepening his life in me." That's it. Every day and everywhere, I am surrounded by a world of God's gifts, all placed right in front of me. Good things that will help me to know God more easily and make a return of love more readily.

All I really have to do is pay attention to the *everyday*, Ignatius says, for this is where God shows up, present and dynamic. Here, he writes, "everything has the potential of calling forth in us a deeper response to our life in God." God's Spirit is with me as I enter into Scripture and worship. God acts through encounters with friends, roommates, colleagues, parents, children, even through strangers.

Even more surprisingly, God reaches me through my own emotions, imagination, ideas, and desires. I can come to know God more deeply by coming to know myself more honestly. I don't have to wander blindly through the maze of questions, guided only by inadequate religious formulas. I may freely ask God to clear the static of "disordered affections," and come close, to guide me now as I pray and watch. Ignatius's devotional workouts help channel my scattered impulses toward stronger, more mature faith in Christ.

I am drawn to the Ignatian way of contemplation in action. It's the art of receptive prayer that moves me toward meaningful, real-time response. When there's a fork in the road and I've got to choose one way or another, Ignatius gives me some helpful tools for sorting through the options.

So what of my young friend Richard? It's as if Ignatius leaned across the span of 450 years and said, "Settle down now, young man. Remember that God is present everywhere and in everything—and in this decision too. You've got two choices here. They're both good ones. So let's break it down. Work the problem." As a business major, Richard finds he is relieved to be handed a method to take the next step along the path that is his alone to discover, trusting God to go with him.

In the same way, I've found that Ignatius's methodical approach to discernment opens up a new confidence in the creative, personal way that I "do" spirituality. I don't have to hit upon that elusive One Perfect Live-or-Die Answer. Instead, making a decision becomes an organic process: I consider the words of Scripture, of trusted family, mentors, and friends. I listen to the counsel of my own emotions and desires. I pray and I ponder. In the end, I can take risks because I trust in God's loving guidance. God is present in everything, just waiting to be found, if only I will wake up, pay attention, and respond from the heart.

Juana Ines de la Cruz c. 1651–1695

Take Delight in God's Beauty—Within You

Grace lies not in your hand, though the

desire to attain it may be your eager errand. . . .

Grace is a gracious gift, not something we are owed.

THE GIGGLING IN THE BACK OF THE CLASS QUIETED as Miss Meier, our junior high Bible teacher, read the morning's installment from *Foxe's Book of Martyrs,* this time a gory tale of a twelve-year-old girl tortured for her faith. What would God demand from us seventh graders? Miss Meier declared that no adolescent pleasure compared to the eternal glories of heaven. Was I willing to consign my worldly treasures—my Nancy Drew mysteries, *Tiger Beat* magazines, Twinkies, and Monkees records—to flames or flood?

Persecuted as a Christian in East Germany, Miss Meier had abandoned her family and medical career to scramble through dark forests and across a swift river, swimming even as border guards shot at her. Miss Meier had escaped the atheistic communists (a miracle!) and was now free to teach part time at our Christian day school.

From all I could see, chances seemed mighty slim that I'd burn at the stake or dodge bullets for Jesus. Nonetheless, I got the message: following Jesus was going to be painful. Miss Meier left me puzzling over some questions. Who were our present-day persecutors in suburban Philadelphia? Was an actual bonfire in their plans? If I gave up my secular rock albums would God let me keep my cat Boots? Specifics aside, Miss Meier left no doubt that the Christian life was seriousness, sacrifice, and spiritual warfare. The desires I felt, the hopes I had, the career I imagined, even the people I loved, were not mine to claim. When Jesus called me to sacrifice, which could be at any moment, I'd better be prepared to offer up my hand to the flame.

Miss Meier never read us the tale of Juana Ines de la Cruz, the feisty Mexican girl with one sustaining passion: knowledge. At three, Juana persuaded an older sister to teach her to read and write. By six, Juana had heard that in Mexico City there was a college where they studied the sciences, prompting Juana to hatch a plan. "I began to slay my poor mother with insistent and annoying pleas, begging her to dress me in men's clothes," she writes, "so that I could enter the University and study."

In the meantime, Juana devoured the books she found in her grandfather's library: literature, science, philosophy, theology, languages. She developed some quirky habits. "I would abstain from eating cheese because I heard tell that it made people stupid," Juana reports, "and the desire to learn was stronger for me than the desire to eat." Whenever she was dissatisfied with her mastery of a certain subject, she'd cut off her hair to punish her own dull-wittedness. A head that was bare of facts should also be bare of glossy curls.

Given her astounding intellectual discipline and drive, Juana's future as an academic was surely guaranteed. Ah, but wait. The era was seventeenth-century Mexico. The authorities were male, traditional Catholic, Spanish colonialists. And the young scholar? She was the daughter of unwed parents, a Spanish military officer and a Mexican-born mother, a nobody from the town of Nepantla, Aztec for "land in the middle." As an illegitimate child, Juana's birth was not even recorded in the church registry. Her very existence was off the books—but not for long.

This girl of the Land in the Middle knew exactly who she was and what she wanted. She also remained a faithful daughter of the church all of her life. Did she wonder if God would demand that she give up her scholarly aspirations? Was she ready to demonstrate her true faith through acts of submission, all in the name of obedience, piety, propriety?

Once Juana finished off her grandfather's entire bibliotheca, the next thing our preteen prodigy had to do was get herself out of Neptlana and find a way to Mexico City, center of her universe. At thirteen she was presented as a lady-in-waiting to the court of the viceroy and vicereine, the sovereigns of Spain who ruled the New World colony. The royal couple happened to love literature, a lucky break for the new maiden who knew that flattery will get you everywhere. Juana composed a series of romantic poems that starred the vicereine herself, a promising start to her literary career.

The viceroy saw opportunity for amusement in his wife's dazzling young companion. He rounded up the forty finest mathematicians, philosophers, historians, and theologians for an erudite showdown. The men quizzed and questioned the girl in a seventeenth-century Battle of the Brains. Confident in her vast knowledge, Juana outwitted and charmed them all. Only sixteen, Juana had achieved worldly sophistication and local fame. "Of all my country, I was the venerated figure," she wrote, "one of those idols that inspire the general applause."

So what would be her next move? More than anything, Juana wanted to live in solitude with the freedom to study undisturbed, to pursue "beauties with which to stock the mind." The royal court's endless rounds of balls, gallantries, and entertainments were a distraction. After the current viceroy's term was up, Juana might not stay on as lady-in-waiting anyway. With sketchy family credentials and no dowry money, respectable marriage was not for her. Juana was left with only one sanctioned path: to become a nun.

Juana states her logic bluntly: "I took the veil although I knew I would find in the religious life many things that would be quite opposed to my character." In spite of the demands of communal convent life, she writes, "it would, given my absolute unwillingness to enter into marriage, be the least unfitting and the most decent state I could choose."

These days, when only 1,200 young women across the United States are preparing to join Catholic religious orders, it's rare to meet a nun, let alone know a young woman who sees the cloister as a career destination. Things were different back in colonial era Mexico, when convents were a huge social and economic presence. There were sixteen convents in Mexico City in 1650, filled with the daughters of society. Though nuns remained under the authority of male clergy, the cloisters were self-contained feminine worlds combining the spiritual life and an honorable vocation. No wonder our young scholar found it the "least unfitting" option.

Juana Ines was possessed of the gift of an extraordinary intellect, and she fully intended to use it. "I do not value treasures or riches; it always gives me more pleasure to put wealth in my thought than thought in my wealth," she wrote.

And so Juana left the realm of viceregal society. As a Catholic sister at the Convent of San Jeronimo, the novice Sor (sister) Juana Ines de la Cruz was required to attend prayer at fixed hours and to contribute some light work as the convent accountant. Other than that, Juana's time was pretty much her own. The monastic rule to eat meals all together wasn't even enforced. Each nun had private living quarters, staffed by servants, complete with kitchen, bath, sleeping quarters and parlor.

What was not to like about the Convent of San Jeronimo? Sor Juana Ines found much of the independence and tranquility she needed to cultivate her "inclination to study." Her own comfy corner cell had two floors; her second-story window featured a view of the Valley of Mexico. There she built up her own personal collection of books, both secular and sacred, works of art, and a variety of musical and scientific instruments. Over time, Juana Ines amassed the largest library in all of Mexico, right there in her convent rooms.

During her years as a nun of the Convent of San Jeronimo, Juana Ines de la Cruz wrote widely: religious and secular plays, verses for dance tunes, sacred poems, love poems, comedies, philosophy, an essay in theology, even an autobiographical defense of the right of women to study. Her works were published and performed. Juana was renowned as the most erudite woman in Mexico before she was even twenty years old. She grew into a great poet and playwright celebrated across the Western hemisphere.

As a cloistered woman, she was never permitted to leave the convent—ever. But the world came to her. Juana corresponded with learned persons across the Spanish dominions and Europe. Visitors, from academics to courtly socialites, came to her *locutory*. Juana's parlor became a kind of literary and philosophical salon where she taught seminars, read her poetry and plays, and debated ideas.

You haven't heard of Sor Juana Ines de la Cruz? You can blame it on centuries of storytellers, the ones who've recounted the intellectual traditions of men and disregarded the silent and silenced contributions of women. Your ignorance is no surprise. Even in her own day, Juana's bold public voice was hushed by bishops and priests. It's been three hundred fifty years since she lived, but it's not too late to bring Juana back. Her words have been here all along.

And what was the nature of Juana's personal life with God, her deeper devotion to Christ? Some dismiss the role of belief in Juana's experience, presuming that she joined the convent purely as a profession. Never did Juana demonstrate excessive piety, notes one biographer. Alongside the fervent nuns of her day, those who composed flowery mystical writing or inflicted harsh self-mortification, Juana was hardly the conventionally submissive sister. This is hardly remarkable, for Juana was always an independent, atypical woman. Why would she express her faith in a typical way?

Sister Juana had other reasons to be wary of wearing her beliefs on her sleeve. The deadly Spanish Inquisition was in full force in colonial Mexico, enforcing the medieval church doctrines and disciplines of the "true faith." God does not want women meddling in writings "that breed arrogance," Juana Ines was warned. To those who urged her to write more explicitly on "sacred matters" Juana replied, "Let those things be left to those who understand them; I want no trouble with the Holy Office."

Better (and safer) to write poetry and drama, which became, for Juana Ines, a literary theology of God's beauty. "Let us rejoice, Beloved," she writes, "and let us go see ourselves in your Beauty." Her deep commitment to God is enfolded in her philosophical writings, her submission to communal life, and within vivid creative writings intended for the wider world. In verse she reflects, "Grace lies not in your hand, though the desire to attain it may be your eager errand. . . . Grace is a gracious gift, not something we are owed." This first woman theologian of the Americas was bound by the narrow constraints of her time. Ultimately, Juana's reverence would mean sacrificial obedience.

❧ ❧ ❧

The final chapter of Juana's story confuses me. It breaks my heart. This is what historians tell us: For years, Juana Ines de la Cruz followed God's call into the scholarly, artistic life, flourishing in knowledge and in renown. And then, abruptly, Juana renounced her public life as an author and took a vow of silence. Her act brings back the dread I felt in Miss Meier's junior high classroom, the fear that God will strip away the very things I love most. I hear protest in Juana Ines's own plaintive words spoken before she went silent, "If my intellect is my own, why must I always find it so keen to harm me?"

Juana Ines gave away all of her beloved books, treasures, and scientific instruments. Why? Did she submit to pressure from church authorities, the men who were severely critical of her expanding renown? Did she experience some kind of conversion, a new call from God? One scholar suggests that, disillusioned, Juana renounced worldly human studies to enter the hushed world of contemplation and charity. Another sees this as a temporary period of intense spiritual devotion promising renewed intellectual work to come. We will never know, for two years after the renunciation of all that she loved, Juana died from an illness while serving for the sick in her own convent.

What, then, do I make of my own gifts, my own desires, in light of Juana's sad end? Does God want what I want—or does admitting to my hopes put me in peril of seeing them crushed? Am I even permitted to have desires for myself? I've known the love of learning, Juana's "natural impulse which God implanted in me." Unlike her, I've had the privilege of attending college and even graduate school (dressed as a woman, no less). Unimpeded, I have indulged my appetite for cheddar cheese and preference for long hair. I'm surrounded by more books than I could ever finish. After years of sketching outlines during stolen hours, I'm writing this very book. Not until now, though, have I dared to claim it. *I am a writer.*

In my mind, the old dark warning remains below the surface: the Christian life is not about following your own longings. It's about giving up the things you want. Be prepared for renunciation. Even as I name my vocation, I back down, lose confidence. Life is brimming with pressing obligations to be met. By the time I take care of the people who need me and satisfy the day's ordinary demands, can I hope that there will be anything left of me?

Tales of saintly, suffering martyrs inspire apprehension and tumult in my heart. Clarity comes through the words of Scripture. There Jesus speaks a deeper, more beautiful truth. "The thief comes only to steal, slaughter, and destroy," he promises. "I've come that they may have life, and have it abundantly" (John 10:10). No, it isn't Jesus who destroys good things. It wasn't God who consigned a twelve-year-old martyr to torment, who stripped Juana of her books or infected her with the plague. Gifts are denied by the thieving power of sin and death, and that's a power that has already been defeated.

Will I claim what I love in this world, knowing that Jesus is my champion? The words of Scripture come back to me: "The Lord your God is with you, the Mighty Warrior who saves. He will take great delight in you; in his love he will no longer rebuke you, but will rejoice over you with singing" (Zephaniah 3:17). The present, mighty, saving God sings over me as he sang over Juana Ines "to make a Heaven of the very Heaven." Because I can believe that good news, I will sing along.

SOPHIE SCHOLL 1921–1943

Knock a Chip Out of the Wall

Such a glorious, sunny day and I must go. But what will my death matter if, because of our actions, thousands of people are wakened and stirred to action?

DO JUSTICE, LOVE MERCY *and walk humbly with God* (Micah 6:8). I'm inspired by the Christians who enact these words of Scripture every single day. The hundreds of lawyers, investigators, and social workers of International Justice Mission who intervene, at great risk, to dismantle human trafficking and forced labor slavery around the world. The 170 Christians who recently walked from Tijuana to Los Angeles on a 150-mile pilgrimage called the El Camino del Inmigrante, an act of solidarity with our immigrant brothers and sisters. Melina, my young friend who made the trek, explains, "Our footsteps were our prayers. Our feet painfully screamed, 'Thy Kingdom come' in an imploration of hope and desperation." Sarah, who took her elite college degree to rural Cameroon, Africa, to labor as a linguist with Wycliffe Bible translators.

Taking a stand for a righteous cause feels good, especially when folks around me are into it too. I sign the petition to end campus sexual assault, host a panel on racial reconciliation, and buy local produce at the Saturday farmer's market. While I admire the passionate people who make a big difference in our troubled society, I know that action requires risk. Risk that, when I'm honest enough to confront it, can stop me in my tracks.

❧ ❧ ❧

Do I dare to change my world in Jesus' name? Would I do what Sophie Scholl did? She was only a university student when she went right up against Adolf Hitler and the entire Third Reich. It's a dramatic tale of bravery, well suited to the big screen. As in many heroic tales, Sophie's story begins quietly. She was born in Germany in 1921, a time of national scarcity, political violence, and unemployment. But as a child living in an out-of-the-way village, Sophie was free to roam the dense forests, pick wild berries, and splash in the river, play music and create art.

Nurtured by their free-thinking Christian parents, the five Scholl children grew up on Socrates, Augustine, and Pascal. They read the texts of Buddhism, Confucius, even the Qur'an. And, of course, they learned the Bible. Verses like James 1:22, "But be ye doers of the word, and not hearers only." The kids learned early on that words must be made real in actions. As the lone pacifist in their tiny conservative hamlet, their father, Robert, admonished them, "What I want for you is to live in uprightness and freedom of spirit, no matter how difficult that proves to be." In fact, this would ultimately cost them everything.

Sophie was only twelve years old when Adolf Hitler came to power in 1933. One by one, the Scholl children joined the Hitler Youth, proud to help Germany achieve prosperity. Sophie relished camping, hiking, and scouting with the Young Girls' League. Her older brother Hans was chosen to carry the flag of his six-hundred-member regiment at the 1936 Nuremberg Nazi Party Convention.

From the very start, Robert opposed the new führer, for he perceived malignant intentions behind Hitler's brash promises. Father and son argued constantly about the Hans's nationalistic enthusiasms.

Robert dreaded what lay ahead, declaring, "If those bastards harm my children in any way, I'll go to Berlin and shoot Hitler."

But soon the children caught on. Hans became disillusioned with the inane drills, paramilitary parades, and vulgar jokes of the Hitler Youth. ("No one had time for a sensible conversation!" he grumbled.) Even little Sophie saw that something was very wrong when two of her Jewish girlfriends were barred from her local Girls' League. As a teenager, Sophie became quite open about her hatred of the aggression of the Third Reich. "I will never understand it; I think it is horrible. Do not say it is for the fatherland," she wrote to her boyfriend, Fritz, an officer in the German army.

The Scholls began to resist the status quo. Sophie was reprimanded for reading banned books. Hans was imprisoned for removing the Nazi emblem from his youth troop's flag. Robert was arrested for calling Hitler names. But the inexorable Nazi terror rolled across mainland Europe and on toward Russia. In 1940 in the midst of war, Sophie Scholl graduated from high school. It would be two wretched years before she could begin her university studies.

Like other German teenagers, Sophie was drafted into Nazi service. She endured her term as a nameless "labor maid" at the unheated, decrepit Krauchenwies castle. (Picture a nightmare version of summer camp.) After a day of mandatory field work, as the other girls gossiped and laughed on their bunks, Sophie pulled the blanket over her head and read Saint Augustine by flashlight. Miserable, she continually repeated a line of Goethe's poetry to herself, "Braving all powers, holding your own."

As she pulled weeds out in the blooming poppy fields, Sophie had plenty of time to reflect. "Isn't it a tremendous enigma and . . . almost frightening, that everything is so beautiful? In spite of the terrible things that are going on," Sophie wrote to a friend that night. Convinced nonetheless that God will always have the last word against violence, Sophie vowed, "I will try to take the victor's side."

On her twenty-first birthday, Sophie was on a train at last, off to begin her college studies alongside her brother at the university in Munich. Hans welcomed Sophie into his band of buddies—Christoph, Willi, and Alexander. The close confidantes shared a love of art, literature, classical music, hiking, philosophical debate—and a fierce opposition to Hitler. But Munich's Maximilian University was no shelter for dissent. It was an intellectual stronghold of National Socialism, governed by a high-ranking SS officer and a site of Nazi book burnings. The four young men were forced to report for regular military drills and spend school vacations as medics in the army. They heard distressing first-hand reports of atrocities from classmates forced to fight on the Eastern front.

As grim news came that members of the Resistance had been captured, Hans felt convicted by the old Scholl family principle: you've got to stand up for what's right, no matter the cost. Hans saw that the Communists were taking a stand. Why not the followers of Jesus? "It's high time that Christians made up their minds to do something!" he said to his friends. "What are we going to show in the way of resistance when all this terror is over?" he asked them. "We will be standing empty-handed. We will have no answer when we are asked: *What did you do about it?*"

This inauspicious group of students determined to fight the Nazi regime together, though their peers, "good citizens" all, unequivocally supported war. Hans, Sophie, Christoph, Willi, and Alexander, along with Professor Kurt Huber, formed a secret group they named the White Rose. They imagined the Third Reich as an enormous stone wall of impossibility. As the White Rose, they would discover ways, however small, to knock chips out of the wall. They believed, with the optimism of youth, that if only their fellow citizens knew the truth about Hitler, things would change; their tangible acts of nonviolent resistance would spark an uprising and end the war. At night they painted the walls of university and public buildings, declaring in large black block letters, "DOWN WITH HITLER!" and "LONG LIVE FREEDOM!"

What else could they do?

The members of the White Rose came from Protestant, Catholic, and Russian Orthodox backgrounds, and they shared the convictions of the Christian faith. As it happened, the inspiration for their boldest action came from a Roman Catholic minister, Bishop Clemens August von Galen. From the pulpit, Galen condemned Nazi eugenics, the program ordering the murder of the mentally ill, physically deformed, and incurably sick. Galen's subversive sermons were transcribed, copied, and circulated secretly by hand—and roused widespread opposition. "Finally someone has the courage to speak," Hans exclaimed, "and all you need is a duplicating machine!"

The White Rose covertly wrote, printed, and distributed thousands of illegal flyers, messages of protest and warning: "We must bring this monster of a state to an end soon." "The war is approaching its certain end." "Hitler cannot win the war—He can only prolong it." They left leaflets in public phone booths, university hallways, and mailboxes. At great risk, they traveled by train to mail anonymous letters from other German cities so that the flyers would bear postmarks from across the country. With a cunning that today's social media gurus would admire, the tiny group created the illusion of a large-scale movement.

Leaders of the Third Reich were desperate to know who was behind the notorious White Rose campaign. The truth came out by chance. On February 18, 1943, Hans and Sophie Scholl stood at the top of a staircase high above the university courtyard just as classes were about to let out. Sophie opened a suitcase of leaflets and emptied it over the balustrade. As hundreds of flyers fluttered down in a blizzard of paper, a janitor stepped out into the hall and saw the brother and sister. He grabbed the pair in a citizen's arrest and consigned them to the Gestapo to be imprisoned and interrogated. Within four short days, Hans, Sophie, and their friend Christoph Probst would be on trial for their lives.

How terrified Sophie must have been. In a private moment, she wrote, "I shall cling to the rope God has thrown me in Jesus Christ, even if my numb hands can no longer feel it." But in the courtroom, without a single witness called in their defense, people say that Sophie, Hans, and Christoph remained calm, composed, clear, unflinching as they were condemned to die. The infamous Nazi judge raged and screamed at the young defendants, roaring until his voice cracked, jumping up again and again in a red-hot frenzy. Standing before him, the twenty-one-year-old Sophie broke in calmly and boldly declared, "Somebody, after all, had to make a start. What we wrote and said is also believed by many others. They just don't dare to express themselves."

The court's guilty verdict was swift and merciless. Spoken after a night of inexplicably calm sleep, Sophie's parting words to her cell mate touch my heart: "Such a glorious, sunny day, and I must go. But how many must die on the battlefields, how many promising young men. . . . What will my death matter if, because of our actions, thousands of people will be awakened and stirred to action!"

As they faced their execution by guillotine on that very same day, Sophie and Hans had only moments to say goodbye to their parents. Holding their hands through the prison bars, Hans reassured them, "I have no hatred. I have put everything, everything behind me." Grasping at something, anything, to comfort her daughter in this heartrending farewell, their mother, Magdelene, said, "Remember, Sophie: *Jesus*." Sophie paused, and then firmly, almost imperiously, her eyes locked on her mother's, replied. "Yes," she said, "but you must remember, too."

The prison warden, awed by their courage, made an exception to allow Hans, Sophie, and Christoph to have one last cigarette together. He heard Christoph say, "I didn't know that dying could be so easy. In a few minutes we meet again in eternity." As he put his head on the block, it is said that Hans cried out in a loud voice, "Long live freedom!"

And that was the end. The Nazi machine continued its killing, undeterred.

❧ ❧ ❧

I can't get through the trailer for the 2005 film *Sophie Scholl: The Final Days* without crying. I'll tell you right now: I am in awe of this girl and her handsome brother. Even from a distance of many decades, I love Sophie and Hans.

But the protective mother in me only wishes that Sophie had kept to herself a bit longer, quiet in her dissent, until the tide turned against the Nazis two years later. Looking back at history, I wonder: What did Sophie and Hans have to show for their bravery? Perhaps they died for nothing. If I could time travel, I might go back to the year Sophie was still a labor maid, reciting Goethe and daydreaming in the poppy fields. I'd slip a secret letter into Sophie's theology book, warning Sophie to keep her head down, to stay hidden under the blankets. To pursue her studies and wait it out. This massive Nazi holocaust is so very far beyond you, I'd write. Look, the war will be over before you're even twenty-five—then you can live your life! You'll have time to make a difference, to rebuild your country.

I have no doubt that Sophie would dismiss my cautionary advice as faithless cowardice. And she would be right. She'd act as a daughter of Robert and Magdalene, the parents who raised their children to follow uprightness and freedom of spirit. It is horrible how many good Christians risk their lives in the war for an outright senseless cause, Sophie lamented, yet "hardly a single person is willing to risk his life to fight Evil. Someone must do it." The undeniable scriptural truth is that *doing* is the heart of *believing*. Faced with evil, the choice was clear. As she contended before the Gestapo judge: "Somebody had to make a start."

There are great stone walls of problems facing us today. Hate surges around us. Refugees, minorities, women, the poor—countless vulnerable ones are at risk here in my own country. When I sense the call to make a change in the world, I am tempted to rationalize my hesitation to respond. I tally up the reasons why a problem is too impenetrable, why democracy should solve it, why any action of mine would be too small.

Then the memory of Sophie Scholl comes back to me. All Sophie could do was paint graffiti and send paper leaflets out into the dark world. I can almost hear the question she asked before she died, "How can we expect righteousness to prevail when there is hardly anyone willing to give himself up to a righteous cause?" How can I attempt any less than to knock just one chip out of the wall? I know that I must be more than a hearer of the Word. I must step forward and make a start.

Conclusion

Resting

Stand at the crossroads and look;

ask for the ancient paths,

ask where the good way is, and walk in it,

and you will find rest for your souls.

Jeremiah 6:16

And so I have arrived. Well, hardly. Pausing to rest along the dusty path, I look up to see another twist in this pilgrim road and a steep climb ahead. I follow the ancient tracks that the saints have made, knowing that they'll lead me to dead ends and confusing detours but, perhaps just around the bend, to some stunning scenic overlook: a glimpse of eternity. Whenever I breathe in the out-of-the-blue glory of a wide horizon, I'm infused with hope and a reassurance that, yes, I am on the good way.

French theologian Henri de Lubac once said that when we meet a saint, we are not discovering at long last an ideal, lived, realized, and fully formed. A saint is not perfect humanity incarnate in one person. "The marvel is of a different order," de Lubac writes. What we find instead is "a new life, a new sphere of existence, with unsuspected depths—but also with a resonance hitherto unknown" to us and now at last revealed.

With a vintage Christian in the lead, I am shown a strange country, a home I originally overlooked, though I find that as soon as I see it, I recognize it as older and truer than anything I have known, a place with claims upon my heart.

De Lubac warns that what I discover is not my loveliest dream. And he is right: I am at once attracted and repelled by the demands of faith. The saints provoke me, disturb me, confuse me—and they sure don't allow me to sit off to the side, safe as a spectator or a cheerleader. They summon me to choose and to act.

Like confident, experienced older brothers and sisters, vintage saints and sinners beckon me into the proven trails they've blazed ahead. If I'll just hold out my hand and follow them, I'll learn the truth of what de Lubac says: "All of a sudden the universe seems different; it is the stage of a vast drama, and we, at its heart, are compelled to play our part." Here is the discovery: a transformative spiritual life is for the likes of me too.

It seems that John's words in Revelation, then, are for you and for me—for all of us: "Here is a call for the endurance of the saints, those who keep the commandments of God and their faith in Jesus" (Revelation 14:12). Along this journey, John says, the saints are just those sinners who endure: the ones who keep God's commandments and hold fast to the faith.

For so long, you and I put off this pilgrimage. We delayed, assuming we'd have to train for holiness and master rigorous ascetic practices, endless prayers, mystical contemplations, and virtuous deeds. Finally get ourselves together. But instead God asks us to simply walk—something that we already know how to do—and so walk into our sainthood, if we will obey, hold fast, endure.

Arriving at yet another crossroads, we stop to look, rubbing our blistered feet and drinking deeply from our water bottles. We ask again for the ancient paths, for the good way—and then we trek on, with a measure of rest in our souls.

Acknowledgments

I OFFER UP MY WARMEST THANKS . . .

To the generations of students who've turned up to meet the saints at Vintage lunches each Friday: for bringing your whole hearts, for asking your questions, for speaking your minds, for showing me faith.

To every Theological Horizons board member, partner, and friend: since 1991 (!) your leadership and your generous support have kept the doors open, put home-cooked meals on the table, and brought these stories, ancient and new, to life.

To Sylvie Greenberg, literary agent extraordinaire: for shepherding this book from start to finish.

To my champions at InterVarsity Press: Helen Lee, Cindy Bunch, Lori Neff, Jeff Crosby, and the entire IVP team. You've envisioned tremendous things for this project—and have brought your many gifts to seeing them realized. (Elissa Schauer, you get a gold medal.)

To Lauren Winner: for unbounded kindness. You taught me to say no, and to start writing.

To Susan Holman and Jennifer Seidel: for venturing into the weeds and leading me out.

To Elena Alba, Katarina Gray, Peter Hartwig, Hannah Grace Martin, Stephen Rooker, and Kate Thorne: for braving an early draft.

To Cameron Archer, Sarah Daubert, Maddy Partridge Green, Betty Li, Camille Loomis, Reilly O'Hara, Olivia Patton, and Melina Rapazzini: for appearing in these pages.

To Brenda Cox and Sarah Munday: for caring about the details.

To the Collegeville Institute, for the transformative writing workshop, and to Robert Benson, Jill Duffield, and the other Cartographers of Grace: for inviting me to be a writer.

To Diana Butler Bass, Catherine and Jerry Capps, Andy Crouch, David Dark, Stephen Garber, Christopher Heuertz, Myra and Bob Marsh, Soong-Chan Rah, James K. A. Smith, Curt Thompson, Margie and Chuck Wright, and Philip Yancey: for lifting me up and cheering me on.

To Ida and Jim Bell, Kathy and Richard Lee, and Trudy Hale: for blissful, sheltered days of creative work.

To Huberta Von Voss Wittig and Peter Wittig: for exemplifying true civility.

To Nichole Flores: for Sor Juana Ines.

To Susan Cunningham: for acting the midwife.

To Greg Breeding and Steve Schoeffel: for creating beautiful things.

To Erica Goldfarb, Bev Wispelwey, and Wendy Baucom: for staying close, for hearing me out.

To Saranell Hartman and Christen Borgman Yates, for keeping things going—with generous spirits.

To Henry, Will, and Nan: for your brilliance and affection. You see this life from the inside; I've done my best to tell the truth.

And, above all, to Charles, my best beloved author of all time. Year after year you've inhabited the stories with me and offered endless grace, love, and cheers. I love you.

In Their Own Words

Recommendations for Further Reading

Søren Kierkegaard

The Prayers of Kierkegaard. Edited by Perry D. LeFevre. Chicago: University of Chicago Press, 1996.

Works of Love. New York: Harper, 2009.

Augustine

Confessions. Translated by Henry Chadwick. Oxford: Oxford University Press, 2009.

Monica: An Ordinary Saint by Gillian Clark. New York: Oxford University Press, 2015.

Thérèse of Lisieux

Story of a Soul: The Autobiography of St. Thérèse of Lisieux. Translated from the original manuscripts by John Clarke, OCD. 3rd ed. Washington, DC: ICS Publications, 1996.

C. S. Lewis

The Chronicles of Narnia. 7 vols. New York: HarperCollins, 1950–1956.

A Grief Observed. New York: HarperOne, 1996.

Surprised by Joy: The Shape of My Early Life. San Diego: Harcourt Brace Jovanovich, 1966.

Henri Nouwen

The Inner Voice of Love: A Journey Through Anguish to Freedom. New York: Doubleday, 1996.

The Spiritual Life: Eight Essential Titles by Henri Nouwen. San Francisco: HarperOne, 2016.

Flannery O'Connor

Flannery O'Connor: Spiritual Writings. Modern Spiritual Masters Series. Maryknoll, NY: Orbis, 2003.

A Prayer Journal. Edited by William Sessions. New York: Farrar, Straus & Giroux, 2013.

Martin Luther

Martin Luther in His Own Words: Essential Writings of the Reformation. Edited by Jack D. Kilcrease and Erwin W. Lutzer. Grand Rapids: Baker Books, 2017.

Table Talk. Edited by Theodore G. Tappert and Helmut T. Lehmann. Luther's Work Book 54. Minneapolis: Fortress, 1967.

Amanda Berry Smith

An Autobiography: The Story of the Lord's Dealings with Mrs. Amanda Smith, the Colored Evangelist; Containing an Account of Her Life Work of Faith, and Her Travels in America, England, Ireland, Scotland, India, and Africa, as an Independent Missionary. Digital edition. Academic Affairs Library: University of North Carolina at Chapel Hill, 1999. http://docsouth.unc.edu/neh/smitham/smith.html.

Dietrich Bonhoeffer

Discipleship. Dietrich Bonhoeffer Works, Vol. 4. Minneapolis: Fortress, 2003.

Life Together and Prayerbook of the Bible. Dietrich Bonhoeffer Works, Vol. 5. Minneapolis: Fortress, 2004.

Strange Glory: A Life of Dietrich Bonhoeffer by Charles Marsh. New York: Knopf, 2014.

A Testament to Freedom: The Essential Writings of Dietrich Bonhoeffer. New York: HarperOne, 2009.

A. W. Tozer

The Best of A. W. Tozer, Books 1 and 2. Compiled by Warren Wiersbe. Chicago: Wingspread, 2007.

The Pursuit of God. Chicago: Wingspread, 2007.

Mother Teresa

Come Be My Light: The Private Writings of the "Saint of Calcutta." Edited by Brian Kolodiejchuk, MC. New York: Doubleday, 2007.

Mother Teresa: In My Own Words. Compiled by José González-Balado. Liguori, MO: Liguori, 1996.

Brother Lawrence

The Practice of the Presence of God: Critical Edition. Translated by Salvatore Sciurba, OCD. Washington, DC: ICS Publications, 1994.

Thomas Merton

The Seven Storey Mountain: An Autobiography of Faith. New York: Harcourt, 1948.

Thomas Merton: Essential Writings. Modern Spiritual Masters Series. Maryknoll, NY: Orbis, 2000.

Benedict and Scholastica

St. Gregory the Great. *The Life of St. Benedict.* Translated and commentary by Terrence G. Kardong. Collegeville, MN: Liturgical Press, 2009.

The Rule of Saint Benedict. Edited by Timothy Fry, OSB. Vintage Spiritual Classics. New York: Vintage Books, 1981.

Fannie Lou Hamer

Fannie Lou Hamer. Testimony Before the Credentials Committee, Democratic National Convention, 1964. Online at www.youtube.com/watch?v=_TchoKJrvFQ.

"'I'm on my way, praise God': Mrs. Hamer's Fight for Freedom," pp. 10-48. In Charles Marsh, *God's Long Summer: Stories of Faith and Civil Rights.* Princeton, NJ: Princeton University Press, 2008.

John Wesley

The Essential Works of John Wesley. Edited by Alice Russie. Uhrichsville, OH: Barbour, 2013.

Susannah Wesley: The Complete Writings. Edited by Charles Wallace Jr. New York: Oxford University Press, 1997.

Francis and Clare of Assisi

Francis and Clare: The Complete Works. Translated by Regis J. Armstrong and Ignatius C. Brady. Classics of Western Spirituality. New York: Paulist Press, 1986.

The Little Flowers of St. Francis of Assisi. Translated by W. Heywood with an introduction by Madeleine L'Engle. New York: Vintage Books, 1998.

Dorothy Day

Dorothy Day: Selected Writings. Edited by Robert Ellsberg. Maryknoll, NY: Orbis, 2005.

Howard Thurman

With Head and Heart: The Autobiography of Howard Thurman. New York: Harcourt Brace Jovanovich, 1979.

Howard Thurman: Essential Writings. Modern Spiritual Masters Series. Maryknoll, NY: Orbis, 2006.

Julian of Norwich

The Complete Julian of Norwich. Edited by Fr. John-Julian, OJN. Paraclete Giants. Brewster, MA: Paraclete, 2009.

The Writings of Julian of Norwich: A Vision Showed to a Devout Woman and A Revelation of Love. Edited by Nicholas Watson and Jacqueline Jenkins. University Park: Pennsylvania State University Press, 2006.

Mary Paik Lee

Quiet Odyssey: A Pioneer Korean Woman in America. Edited by Sucheng Chan. Seattle: University of Washington Press, 1990.

Aelred of Rievaulx

The Life of Aelred of Rievaulx, and the Letter to Maurice by Walter Daniel. Collegeville, MN: Cistercian, 1994.

Spiritual Friendship. Translated by Lawrence C. Braceland, SJ. Edited by Marsha L. Dutton. Collegeville, MN: Cistercian, 2010.

Ignatius of Loyola

Draw Me into Your Friendship: A Literal Translation and a Contemporary Reading of the Spiritual Exercises by David Fleming, SJ. Boston: Institute of Jesuit Sources, 1996.

Juana Ines de la Cruz

Selected Works. Translated by Edith Grossman. New York: W. W. Norton, 2014.

Sophie Scholl

Inge Scholl, *The White Rose: Munich, 1942–1943.* 2nd ed. Middletown, CT: Wesleyan University Press, 1983.

Books I Keep Going Back To . . .

All Saints: Daily Reflections on Saints, Prophets and Witnesses for Our Time by Robert Ellsberg. New York: Crossroad, 1997.

Devotional Classics: Selected Readings for Individuals and Groups. Edited by Richard J. Foster and James Bryan Smith. Grand Rapids: Zondervan, 2005.

My Life with the Saints by James Martin, SJ. Chicago: Loyola Press, 2007.

Spiritual Classics: Selected Readings for Individuals and Groups on the Twelve Spiritual Disciplines. Edited by Richard J. Foster and Emilie Griffin. San Francisco: HarperOne, 2000.

For more resource suggestions, go to karenwrightmarsh.com.

Additionally, head to theologicalhorizons.org for vintage readings, curriculum, video, and many other resources. Sign up as a member and you'll get all the good stuff. Do you have books, sources, or insights to share? Let me hear from you: Karen@theologicalhorizons.org.

Conversation Starters

- Dorothy Day said, "Don't call me a saint. I don't want to be dismissed so easily." What do you think she had in mind when she said that? What makes us bristle at the term *saint*?
- The term "sinner-saint" is an uncommon mashup—but for the purposes of this conversation, let's use it. How does this term "sinner-saint" help you understand or redefine the word *saint*?
- Which familiar sinner-saint have you come to know in a new way? What surprised you about that person? What question do you wish you could ask him or her?
- Identify a strength that you admire in one of the sinner-saints. How did he or she develop that strength?
- Identify a weakness you see in a particular sinner-saint. How did that weakness affect his or her relationship with God? With other people?
- Who have been your spiritual role models throughout life? What attracted you to them?
- Søren Kierkegaard confesses that baring the intimacies of his life with God is "so difficult, so difficult." What makes discussing our spiritual lives with others so difficult? What would make it easier?
- What portrayal or understanding of God did you find encouraging? What idea about God did you find discomfiting?

- Several sinner-saints experienced dramatic encounters with God. What do you make of these kinds of intense experiences? How have you encountered God in your own story?
- What does "wholehearted Christianity" mean to you?
- Which sinner-saint disturbed or irritated you? Why? What have you learned from that saint?
- Which story of doubt or struggle challenged you most? Why?
- Lauren Winner writes, "I don't read about the saints in order to imitate them. I read about the saints because they show me something about myself." What do these sinner-saints show you about yourself?
- Henri de Lubac says that saints reveal "a new life, a new sphere of existence, with unsuspected depths." What new aspects of life do you perceive because of the sinner-saints in this book?
- What holds you back from calling yourself a saint? What holds you back from calling yourself a sinner?
- Revelation 14:12 says, "Here is a call for the endurance of the saints, those who keep the commandments of God and their faith in Jesus." What kind of endurance is required of a saint? How might you develop that endurance?
- Think about the image of a crossroads in Jeremiah 6:16: "This is what the Lord says: 'Stand at the crossroads and look; ask for the ancient paths, ask where the good way is, and walk in it, and you will find rest for your souls.'" In what ways are you at a crossroads in your life right now? What ancient paths might you follow tomorrow? How could you take the first step? What might it mean to find rest for your soul?

Notes

vi *God creates out of nothing*: Søren Kierkegaard, *Kierkegaard's Journals and Notebooks*, vol. 2, *Journals EE-KK* (Princeton, NJ: Princeton University Press, 2015), 96.

Introduction

5 *Expect great things*: William Carey, "William Carey: Father of Modern Protestant Missions," www.christianitytoday.com/history/people/missionaries/william-carey.html, accessed December 31, 2016.

6 *quotidian mysteries*: Kathleen Norris, *The Quotidian Mysteries: Laundry, Liturgy, and "Women's Work"* (Mahwah, NJ: Paulist Press, 1998).

7 *Don't call me a saint*: Robert Ellsberg, "All Are Called to Be Saints," *The Catholic Worker*, May 2015, 1, 5, www.catholicworker.org/pages/ellsberg-called-saints.html.

8 *For me to be a saint*: Thomas Merton, *New Seeds of Contemplation* (New York: New Directions, 1961), 31.

Søren Kierkegaard

11 *Teach me, O God*: Søren Kierkegaard, in *The Prayers of Kierkegaard*, ed. Perry D. LeFevre (Chicago: University of Chicago Press, 1956), 27.

12 *monstrously brooding*: Ibid., 126.

13 *It is the mark of an educated mind*: Aristotle, www.uky.edu/~eushe2/quotations/aristotle.html, accessed December 31, 2016.

What I really lack: Kierkegaard, *Prayers of Kierkegaard*, 129-30.

seriously a Christian: Ibid., 132.

14 *indescribable joy*: Ibid., 219.

parson's trash: Ibid., 136.

15 *The function of prayer*: Kierkegaard, quoted in Andrew Gregory, *The Presocratics and the Supernatural: Magic, Philosophy and Science in Early Greece* (London: A&C Black, 2013), 92.

16 *so difficult*: Kierkegaard, *Prayers of Kierkegaard*, 197.

My inwardness: Ibid.

It is wonderful: Ibid., 202.

The best help in all action: Ibid., ii.

Father in Heaven: Ibid., 13.

Augustine

18 *number one party school*: Seth Cline, "Playboy: UVA Is Nation's Top Party School," USnews.com, September 26, 2012, www.usnews.com /news/articles/2012/09/26/playboy-uva-is-nations-top-party-school -playboy-uva-is-nations-top-party-school.

19 *I came to Carthage*: Andrew Knowles and Pachomios Penkett, *Augustine and His World* (Downers Grove, IL: InterVarsity Press, 2004), 39.

muddy carnal concupiscence: Augustine, *Confessions* (Oxford: Oxford University Press, 2008), 25.

20 *Let him be where he is*: Augustine, *Devotional Classics: Selected Readings for Individuals and Groups*, ed. Richard J. Foster, rev. ed. (Grand Rapids: Zondervan, 2005), 51.

By the guidance of wisdom: Marcus Tullius Cicero, in *Thoughts of Cicero*, ed. R. Griffiths (at the Dunciad in St. Paul's Church-yard, 1750), 43.

Prudence, reason and reflection: Ibid., 359.

21 *Of what profit*: Augustine, *The Confessions of St. Augustine, Bishop of Hippo*, ed. J. G. Pilkington (Edinburgh: T&T Clark, 1876), 80.

God, grant me chastity: Augustine, *Devotional Classics*, 146.

Let it be now: Ibid., 151.

I felt that I was still: Peter Brown, *Augustine of Hippo* (Berkeley: University of California Press, 1969), 108.

21 *Take it and read*: Augustine, *Devotional Classics,* 59.

22 *Not in reveling*: *Augustine Through the Ages: An Encyclopedia*, ed. Allan Fitzgerald and John C. Cavadini (Grand Rapids: Eerdmans, 1999), 68.

23 *God, You have formed us for Yourself*: Augustine, *Confessions* (London: Penguin, 1961), 21.

You, O Lord, never ceased: Augustine, *Devotional Classics,* 57.

Thérèse of Lisieux

26 *Go . . . Go*: Philip Zaleski, "The Love of St. Thérèse," *First Things*, December 2004, www.firstthings.com/article/2004/12/the-love-of-saint-thrse.

27 *like eating too many marshmallows*: Ibid.

furnace of divine love: Thérèse of Lisieux, in *Story of a Soul: The Autobiography of St. Thérèse of Lisieux*, trans. John Clarke, OCD, 3rd ed. (Washington, DC: ICS Publications, 2005).

My God, I choose all: Brother Francis Mary, *St. Therese: Doctor of the Little Way* (New Bedford, MA: Academy of the Immaculate, 1998), 14.

28 *Perhaps none heard it*: Thérèse of Lisieux, *Thoughts of Saint Thérèse* (Rockford, IL: Tan Books, 1915), 68.

besprinkles: Ibid., 69.

Jesus does not demand: Thérèse of Lisieux, in Albert Ayers Forrester, *Essays and Questions on Catholic Theology* (Bloomington, IL: Xlibris, 2013), 361.

When I suffer much: Thérèse of Lisieux, *Thoughts of Saint Thérèse,* 142.

29 *Out of love I will suffer*: Thérèse, quoted in Hans Urs von Balthazar, *Two Sisters of the Spirit: Thérèse of Lisieux and Elizabeth of the Trinity* (San Francisco: Ignatius Press, 1992), 250.

30 *In everything I must find self-denial*: Thérèse of Lisieux, *Thoughts of Saint Thérèse,* 70.

C. S. Lewis

32 *I believe in no religion*: C. S. Lewis, *Letters of C. S. Lewis,* ed. W. H. Lewis (San Diego: Houghton Mifflin Harcourt, 2003), 52.

32 *Faith is the great cop-out*: Richard Dawkins, quoted in Alistair McGrath, *Christianity: An Introduction* (Oxford: Blackwell, 2006), 102.

33 *not the religious type*: C. S. Lewis, in Alan Jacobs, *The Narnian: The Life and Imagination of C. S. Lewis* (San Francisco: HarperSanFrancisco, 2005), xix.

reluctant convert: Ibid., 129.

34 *not only could he see the sun*: In *The Quotable Lewis,* ed. Wayne Martindale and Jerry Root (Carol Stream, IL: Tyndale House, 1989), 99.

35 *Our feeblest contemplations*: Carl Sagan, *Cosmos* (New York: Ballantine Books, 1985), 1.

good, good sound: C. S. Lewis, *A Grief Observed* (Grand Rapids: Zondervan, 2001), 64.

"Dearest daughter," Aslan says: C. S. Lewis, *The Horse and His Boy* (Grand Rapids: Zondervan, 2000), 201.

Henri Nouwen

37 *steep, savage hill*: Henry Wiencek, *Master of the Mountain: Thomas Jefferson and His Slaves* (London: Macmillan, 2012), 3.

38 *like fertile ground*: Henri J. M. Nouwen, *The Inner Voice of Love: A Journey Through Anguish to Freedom* (New York: Doubleday, 1996), 117.

Who am I?: Henri Nouwen, in *Henri Nouwen: Writings Selected with an Introduction by Robert A. Jonas* (Maryknoll, NY: Orbis, 1988), 25.

39 *Determine never to be idle*: Thomas Jefferson, *The Jeffersonian Cyclopedia: A Comprehensive Collection of the Views of Thomas Jefferson* (London: Funk and Wagnalls, 1900), 413.

habitual, almost neurotic need: Robert A. Jonas, in *Henri Nouwen,* xxxiv.

At the core of my faith: Ibid., 24.

That's not very easy: Ibid.

40 *quiet village living*: Henri J. M. Nouwen, *The Road to Daybreak: A Spiritual Journey* (New York: Doubleday, 1988), 8.

I am a very weak: Nouwen, *Henri Nouwen*, xxxii.

41 *Aren't you, like me*: Henri J. M. Nouwen, *Life of the Beloved: Spiritual Living in a Secular World* (New York: Crossroad, 2002), 35.

Flannery O'Connor

43 *by bus or buzzard*: Flannery O'Connor, in *Flannery O'Connor: Spiritual Writings*, ed. Robert Ellsberg (Maryknoll, NY: Orbis, 2003), 21.

Because I'm good at it: Joy Williams, "Stranger Than Paradise," a review of *Flannery: A Life of Flannery O'Connor* by Brad Gooch, *New York Times Sunday Book Review*, March 1, 2009.

I do not mean to be clever: Flannery O'Connor, *A Prayer Journal* (New York: Farrar, Straus & Giroux, 2013), 6.

44 *Please help me dear God*: Ibid., 10.

She was a plain sort of young, unmarried girl: Williams, "Stranger Than Paradise."

very muddy and manuery: O'Connor, in Ellsberg, *Flannery O'Connor*, 23.

I have enough energy: Flannery O'Connor, *The Habit of Being: Letters of Flannery O'Connor*, ed. Sally Fitzgerald (London: Macmillan, 1988), xvi.

45 *In the woods*: O'Connor, in Ellsberg, *Flannery O'Connor*, 124.

typical Southern sense: O'Connor, in Fitzgerald, *Habit of Being*, 548.

idiot legislature: Ibid., 318.

46 *I measure God*: Ibid., 430.

it cuts with the sword: Ibid., 411.

This is the central Christian mystery: Flannery O'Connor, "The Church and the Fiction Writer," *America Magazine*, March 30, 1957, www.americamagazine.org/issue/100/church-and-fiction-writer.

Dear God, I cannot love: O'Connor, *Prayer Journal*, 3.

47 *Oh Lord, make me a mystic*: Ibid., 38.

Please help me: Ibid., 4.

I don't want to be doomed: Ibid., 35.

Martin Luther

49 *To cry unto the Lord*: Martin Luther, in David F. Wells, *God in the Wasteland: The Reality of Truth in a World of Fading Dreams* (Grand Rapids: Eerdmans, 1995), 128.

50 *When I realized*: Quoted in Richard H. Schmidt, *God Seekers: Twenty Centuries of Christian Spiritualities* (Grand Rapids: Eerdmans, 2008), 150.

51 *There is no more lovely*: Quoted in Steven W. Smith and Gary Chapman, *Marriage* (Downers Grove, IL: InterVarsity Press, 2010), 42.

weapons of death: Richard Marius, *Martin Luther: The Christian Between God and Death* (Cambridge, MA: Belknap, 1999), 439.

The Christian should: Luther, in *Faith and Freedom: An Invitation to the Writings of Martin Luther*, ed. John F. Thornton and Susan Varenne (New York: Vintage, 2002), 302.

52 *I shall not die*: Marius, *Martin Luther*, 439.

the worst and saddest: Martin Luther, *Luther: Letters of Spiritual Counsel*, ed. T. G. Tappert (Vancouver: Regent College Publishing, 2003), 95.

we imagine: Ibid.

You must learn: Martin Luther, in Barbara Owen, "Luther's Answers to Anxiety," *The Lutheran Witness* 20, no. 4 (2001): 10.

Amanda Berry Smith

55 *Have the ambition to lean in*: Sheryl Sandberg, *Lean In: Women, Work, and the Will to Lead* (New York: Alfred A. Knopf, 2013), 25-26.

56 *Please ask yourself*: Ibid., 26.

57 *I always had a fear*: Amanda Berry Smith, *An Autobiography: The Story of the Lord's Dealings with Mrs. Amanda Smith, the Colored Evangelist: Containing an Account of Her Life Work of Faith, and Her Travels in America, England, Ireland, Scotland, India, and Africa, as an Independent Missionary* (Chicago: Meyer & Brother, 1893), 80. The online edition of this book has been produced by the Emory University Digital Library Publications Program: https://archive.org/stream/04073779.4704.emory.edu/04073779_4704#page/n7/mode/2up.

I will pray once more: Ibid., 46.

I don't know why: Ibid., 79.

58 *I suppose people thought*: Ibid.

Oh! Lord: Ibid., 111.

I opened my Bible: Ibid.

59 *give me complete victory*: Ibid.

especial manifestation: Ibid.

if Thou wilt help me: Ibid.

mighty skimpey: Ibid., 156.

Mrs. Smith is from New York: Ibid., emphasis added.

Oh, my heart fell down: Ibid.

Now, my child: Ibid.

I seemed to lose sight: Ibid., 157.

Dietrich Bonhoeffer

62 *O, Lord, let my soul*: Shane Claiborne, Jonathan Wilson-Hartgrove, and Enuma Okoro, *Common Prayer: A Liturgy for Ordinary Radicals* (Grand Rapids: Zondervan, 2010), 49.

63 *At the threshold of the new day*: Dietrich Bonhoeffer, *Life Together* (San Francisco: HarperSanFrancisco, 1954), 43.

64 *Everything depends on the urgent*: Dietrich Bonhoeffer, quoted in Charles Marsh, *Strange Glory: A Life of Dietrich Bonhoeffer* (New York: Knopf, 2014), 243.

lightning flash: Ibid., 255.

65 *how beautiful this world can be*: Dietrich Bonhoeffer, *Letters and Papers from Prison* (Minneapolis: Fortress, 2015), 142.

Still is the world: Ibid., 142-43.

despite everything: Ibid., 200.

nauseating burden: Ibid.

66 *Who am I*: Ibid., 448-49.

at an infinite distance: Dietrich Bonhoeffer, in Charles Marsh, *Reclaiming Dietrich Bonhoeffer: The Promise of His Theology* (Oxford: Oxford University Press, 1996), 154.

unreservedly in life's duties: Bonhoeffer, in *Theology and the Practice of Responsibility: Essays on Dietrich Bonhoeffer*, ed. Wayne W. Floyd and Charles Marsh (London: Trinity Press International, 1994), 279.

67 *They mock me*: Bonhoeffer, *Letters and Papers from Prison*, 449.

67 *it is grace*: Dietrich Bonhoeffer, *Life Together: Prayerbook of the Bible* (Minneapolis: Fortress, 1996), 30.

A. W. Tozer

69 *I was little better than a pagan*: A. W. Tozer, in Lyle W. Dorsett, *A Passion for God: The Spiritual Journey of A. W. Tozer* (Chicago: Moody Publishers, 2008), 106.

70 *pure Pennsylvaniaish*: Ada Pfautz Tozer, quoted in ibid., 127.

Save me from the bondage: A. W. Tozer, in ibid., 65-68.

Lay Thy terror: Ibid., 66.

71 *prayer pants*: Ibid., 121.

72 *My husband was so close*: Ada Pfautz Tozer, in ibid., 366.

I've had a lonely life: A. W. Tozer, in ibid., 16.

73 *I have never been happier*: Ada Pfautz Tozer, in ibid., 409.

lonely valleys of soul poverty: From "The Blessedness of Possessing Nothing," in A. W. Tozer, *The Pursuit of God* (Middletown, DE: CreateSpace, 2013), 15.

sinner, writ large: Paul Elie, *A Tremor of Bliss: Contemporary Writers on the Saints* (New York: Harcourt, Brace, 1994), xxi.

Mother Teresa

75 *Christ is in the poor*: Mother Teresa, *Mother Teresa: Essential Writings* (Maryknoll, NY: Orbis, 2001), 119-20.

In my soul: Mother Teresa, in *Come Be My Light: The Private Writings of the "Saint of Calcutta,"* ed. Brian Kolodiejchuk, MC (New York: Doubleday, 2009), 192.

76 *I don't pray*: Ibid., 193.

a fanatic, a fundamentalist: Christopher Hitchens, "Mommie Dearest," *Slate*, October 20, 2003, www.slate.com/articles/news_and_politics/fighting_words/2003/10/mommie_dearest.html.

As far as we know: Kolodiejchuk, *Come Be My Light*, 326.

If you could know how happy: Ibid., 18.

77 *Wouldst thou not*: Ibid., 48.

77 *The thought of eating*: Ibid., 49.

call within a call: Mother Teresa, *Mother Teresa*, 30.

Come, come, carry Me: Kolodiejchuk, *Come Be My Light*, 98.

On Tuesday evening: Ibid., 121.

78 *I wouldn't do that for a million*: James Martin, *My Life with the Saints* (Chicago: Loyola Press, 2006), 164.

In order to be a saint: Mother Teresa, *Mother Teresa*, 131.

I am told: Kolodiejchuk, *Come Be My Light*, 187.

I find no words: Ibid., 192.

79 *unwanted, unloved*: Ibid., 4.

80 *Without Christ*: David Livingstone, quoted in *Draper's Book of Quotations for the Christian World*, comp. Edythe Draper (Carol Stream, IL: Tyndale House, 1992), 207.

Find your own Calcutta: Mother Teresa, in Robert Ellsberg, *All Saints: Daily Reflections on Saints, Prophets, and Witnesses for Our Time* (New York: Crossroad, 1997), 393.

We can do no great: Ibid.

Brother Lawrence

82 *great awkward fellow*: Brother Lawrence, *Practicing the Presence of God*, trans. Robert J. Edmonson, with an introduction and notes by Tony Jones (Brewster, MA: Paraclete, 2007), 44.

83 *I am in the hands*: Ibid., 15.

I resolved to give: Ibid., 73.

84 *It is enough for me to pick up but a straw*: Quoted in Mark Galli, *131 Christians Everyone Should Know* (Nashville: B&H, 2010), 271.

We must make our faith alive: Brother Lawrence, *Practicing the Presence of God*, 124.

singular wisdom: Quoted in ibid., 122.

85 *Think often about God*: Ibid., 88.

establish an unaccustomed habit: James Clear, "How Long Does It Actually Take to Form a New Habit?," *The Huffington Post* (blog), April

10, 2014, www.huffingtonpost.com/james-clear/forming-new-habits_b_5104807.html.

85 *One is not a saint all of a sudden*: Brother Lawrence, *Practicing the Presence*, 85.

a crowd of unruly thoughts: Ibid., 125.

86 *his perseverance was rewarded*: Quoted in ibid.

I no longer believe: Ibid., 134.

Thomas Merton

90 *powerful feeling*: Dalai Lama, in *Thomas Merton by Those Who Knew Him Best*, ed. Paul Wilkes (New York: Harper & Row, 1984), 171.

I believe in nothing: Thomas Merton, quoted in Jim Forest, *Living with Wisdom: A Life of Thomas Merton* (Maryknoll, NY: Orbis, 1991), 15.

beer, bewilderment and sorrow: Ibid., 31.

91 *a noisy and dramatic*: Ibid., 46.

from His own immense: Thomas Merton, *The Seven Storey Mountain* (New York: Harcourt, Brace, 1948), 22.

to disappear into God: Thomas Merton, *The Sign of Jonas* (New York: Harcourt, Brace, 1953), 18.

92 *reserved for a small class*: Merton, in William H. Shannon, *Thomas Merton's Paradise Journey: Writings on Contemplation* (London: Bloomsbury, 2010), 26.

this is so simple: Merton, in *Thomas Merton: Essential Writings*, ed. Christine M. Bochen (Maryknoll, NY: Orbis, 2000), 84.

Love sails me around: Merton, in Forest, *Living with Wisdom*, 97.

93 *There are no strangers*: Merton, in Bochen, *Thomas Merton: Essential Writings*, 92.

the gate of heaven: Merton, in *Thomas Merton, Spiritual Master: The Essential Writings*, ed. Lawrence Cunningham (Mahwah, NJ: Paulist Press, 1992), 146.

as brothers and as builders: Merton, in Bochen, *Thomas Merton: Essential Writings*, 148.

93 *He is more my brother*: Merton, in John Dear, *Thomas Merton Peacemaker: Meditations on Merton, Peacemaking, and the Spiritual Life* (Maryknoll, NY: Orbis, 2015), 78.

94 *What we are asked*: Merton, in Forest, *Living with Wisdom*, 216.

My attitude toward Christianity: Dalai Lama, *Spiritual Advice for Buddhists and Christians* (London: A&C Black, 1998), 22.

95 *We do not want to be beginners*: Merton, in Richard J. Foster, *Celebration of Discipline: The Path to Spiritual Growth* (Grand Rapids: Zondervan, 1988), 2.

Benedict and Scholastica

97 *dull cycle of studying*: Stephen A. Macchia, *Crafting a Rule of Life: An Invitation to the Well-Ordered Way* (Downers Grove, IL: InterVarsity Press, 2012), 16.

98 *place of my beloved solitude*: Avril Maddrell, Veronica della Dora, Alessandro Scafi, and Heather Walton, *Christian Pilgrimage, Landscape and Heritage: Journeying to the Sacred* (Abingdon-on-Thames, UK: Routledge, 2014), 91.

a school for the Lord's service: Benedict of Nursia, in Jonathan Wilson-Hartgrove, *The Rule of Saint Benedict: A Contemporary Paraphrase* (Brewster, MA: Paraclete, 2012), 5.

99 *Seeking his workers*: Benedict, in Robert Benson, *A Good Life: Benedict's Guide to Everyday Joy* (Brewster, MA: Paraclete, 2004), 1.

102 *All must be given*: Joan Chittister, *Wisdom Distilled from the Daily: Living the Rule of St. Benedict Today* (New York: HarperCollins, 1991), 186.

no one should look after himself: Benedict, in Wilson-Hartgrove, *Rule of Saint Benedict*, 107.

It is difficult to examine: Luke Timothy Johnson, in Sheron Patterson, "Perkins Lecturer Urges Knowing When—and When Not—to Speak Up," The United Methodist Church of North Texas, March 15, 2012, www.northtexasumc.org/2012/03/perkins_lecturer_urges_knowing_when_and_when_not_to_speak_up.

break the cycle of incessant chatter: Ibid.

One strategy is to recover: Ibid.

103 *like a communion with the Lord*: Martha Miller, "Virginia's Cheesemaking Nuns Keep Their Gouda in the Red (Wax)," *Washington Post*, July 3, 2012, www.washingtonpost.com/lifestyle/food/virginias-cheesemaking-nuns-keep-their-gouda-in-the-red-wax/2012/07/02/gJQASNxzKW_story.html?utm_term=.c1775b879f81.

Fannie Lou Hamer

105 *beloved community*: Charles Marsh, *The Beloved Community: How Faith Shapes Social Justice, from the Civil Rights Movement to Today* (New York: Basic Books, 2008), 4.

the lady who sings: Charles Marsh, *God's Long Summer: Stories of Faith and Civil Rights* (Princeton, NJ: Princeton University Press, 1999), 17.

sick and tired: Jerry DeMuth, "Fannie Lou Hamer: Tired of Being Sick and Tired," *The Nation*, April 2, 2009, www.thenation.com/article/fannie-lou-hamer-tired-being-sick-and-tired.

I guess if I'd had any sense: Marsh, *God's Long Summer*, 12.

106 *I made up my mind*: Ibid., 16.

Singing brings out: Ibid., 22.

but if you are not putting: Ibid., 25.

107 *Mississippi Freedom Democratic Party*: Ibid., 33.

that illiterate woman: Ibid., 38.

108 *I question America*: Ibid.

Why not follow somebody: Ibid., 24.

109 *Christ was a revolutionary person*: Ibid., 33.

John Wesley

112 *absolute impossibility of being*: John Wesley, in *John Wesley*, introduced by Albert C. Outler (Oxford: Oxford University Press, 1980), 7.

they could not be saved: John Wesley, *The Essential Works of John Wesley*, ed. Alice Russie (Uhrichsville, OH: Barbour, 2011), 48.

113 *It was as if the great deep*: John Wesley, *An Extract of the Rev. Mr. John Wesley's Journal from His Embarking for Georgia to His Return to London* (London: G. Whitfield, 1797), 21.

Was you not afraid: Ibid., 22.

114 *I went to America*: Wesley, *John Wesley*, 44.

I was indeed fighting: John Wesley, quoted in Mark Galli, *131 Christians Everyone Should Know* (Nashville: Holman, 2000), 182.

I felt my heart: Wesley, in Robert Ellsberg, *All Saints: Daily Reflections on Saints, Prophets, and Witnesses for Our Time* (New York: Crossroad, 1998), 263.

Love is the highest gift: John Wesley, quoted in *Devotional Classics: Revised Edition: Selected Readings for Individuals and Groups*, ed. Richard Foster (Grand Rapids: Zondervan, 2005), 259.

115 *The whole world*: Wesley, in Ellsberg, *All Saints*, 264.

Do all the good you can: Wesley, in Galli, *131 Christians*, 183.

Francis and Clare of Assisi

118 *king of the youth*: Jacques Le Goff, *Saint Francis of Assisi* (Hove, UK: Psychology Press, 2004), 27.

Francis, rebuild my house: Jon M. Sweeney, *Francis and Clare: A True Story* (Brewster, MA: Paraclete, 2007), 41.

120 *naive, almost manic imitation*: Ibid., 83.

What once appeared: Francis, in *The Life of S. Francis of Assisi*, trans. Candide Chalippe (Montreal: D. & J. Sadlier, 1889), 353.

121 *Jongleurs de Dieu*: Sweeney, *Francis and Clare*, 96.

soothing, burning, and penetrating: Joan Acocella, "Rich Man, Poor Man: The Radical Visions of St. Francis," *New Yorker*, January 14, 2013.

Dorothy Day

125 *Forster*: Dorothy Day, *The Long Loneliness* (New York: HarperCollins, 1952), 120.

126 *I am surprised*: Robert Coles, *Dorothy Day: A Radical Devotion* (Boston: Da Capo, 1989), 45.

Religion is the opiate: Ibid.

I felt I was betraying: Day, *Long Loneliness*, 144.

127 *a society where it is easier*: "The Aims and Means of the Catholic Worker," *The Catholic Worker*, May 2016, www.catholicworker.org/cw-aims-and-means.html.

127 *political holiness*: Robert Ellsberg, *All Saints: Daily Reflections on Saints, Prophets, and Witnesses for Our Time* (New York: Crossroad, 1998), 519.

128 *plain and simple*: Dorothy Day, "Room for Christ," *The Catholic Worker*, December 2, 1945, www.catholicworker.org/dorothyday/articles/416.html.

we will be judged: Christine M. Bochen, *The Way of Mercy* (Maryknoll, NY: Orbis, 2016).

we must keep repeating: Peter Day, *On Pilgrimage: Dorothy Day* (New York: Bloomsbury T&T Clark, 1999), 177.

Don't call me a saint: Robert Ellsberg, "All Are Called to Be Saints," *The Catholic Worker*, May 2015, www.catholicworker.org/pages/ellsberg-called-saints.html.

The coat which hangs in your closet: Basil of Caeserea, in Billy Kangas, "Teachings of the Early Church Fathers on Poverty and Wealth," *Patheos*, August 25, 2012, www.patheos.com/blogs/billykangas/2012/08/teachings-of-the-early-church-fathers-on-poverty-wealth.html.

129 *People never mean*: Day, in Coles, *Dorothy Day*, 36.

Howard Thurman

132 *The very roots of my being*: Howard Thurman, in Quinton Dixie and Peter Eisenstadt, *Visions of a Better World: Howard Thurman's Pilgrimage to India and the Origins of African American Nonviolence* (Boston: Beacon Press, 2011), 10.

Look up always: Mark R. Bradshaw-Miller, "The Life and Witness of Howard Thurman," a sermon at Westminster Presbyterian Church, February 5, 2006, http://westminstersermons.blogspot.com/2006/02/life-and-witness-of-howard-thurman.html.

133 *If you are trying to get out*: Thurman, in Dixie and Eisenstadt, *Visions of a Better World*, 12.

to the stranger: Ibid., 13.

You are not slaves: Ibid., 6.

the genius of the religion: Howard Thurman, in *Howard Thurman: Essential Writings*, ed. Luther E. Smith Jr. (Maryknoll, NY: Orbis, 2006), 15.

How can I believe: Ibid., 14.

134 *You have lived*: Dixie and Eisenstadt, *Visions of a Better World*, 182.

134 *What do you think*: Howard Thurman, *With Head and Heart: The Autobiography of Howard Thurman* (Boston: Houghton Mifflin Harcourt, 1981), 134-35.

135 *it may be through the Negroes*: Dixie and Eisenstadt, *Visions of a Better World*, xii.

It was not only driving uphill: Jean Burden, "Howard Thurman," *ChickenBones*, www.nathanielturner.com/howardthurman.htm. Accessed February 6, 2017.

136 *What is the word*: Howard Thurman, *Jesus and the Disinherited* (Boston: Beacon Press, 2012), 13.

Don't ask: Quoted in Gil Baillie, *Violence Unveiled: Humanity at the Crossroads* (New York: Crossroad, 1995), xv.

Ultimately there is only: Howard Thurman, *A Strange Freedom: The Best of Howard Thurman on Religious Experience and Public Life*, ed. Walter Earl Fluker and Catherine Tumber (Boston: Beacon Press, 2014), 184.

137 *How indescribably wonderful*: Ibid.

Julian of Norwich

140 *maid named Alice*: from the introduction to *The Shewings of Julian of Norwich*, ed. Georgia Ronan Crampton (Kalamazoo, MI: Medieval Institute Publications, 1994).

a certeyn creature: Ibid.

142 *What is this*: Julian, in Frederick S. Roden, *Love's Trinity: A Companion to Julian of Norwich: Long Text with a Commentary* (Collegeville, MN: Liturgical Press, 2009), 15.

evencristen: Denys Turner, *Julian of Norwich, Theologian* (New Haven, CT: Yale University Press, 2011), xviii.

143 *unpossible to thee is not*: Ibid., 19.

All shall be well: Julian, in Roden, *Love's Trinity*, 98.

144 *pious periscopes*: Turner, *Julian of Norwich*, 18.

give us more light and solace: Julian of Norwich, *Revelations of Divine Love: Unabridged Contemporary English Edition*, trans. Fr. John-Julian, OJN (Brewster, MA: Paraclete, 2011), x.

Mary Paik Lee

146 *Life in America*: Mary Paik Lee, *Quiet Odyssey: A Pioneer Korean Woman in America* (Seattle: University of Washington Press, 1990), 128.

These things I've written: Ibid., xiii.

147 *God must surely be leading*: Ibid., 113.

148 *Such strong quiet courage*: Ibid., 12.

We must have been: Ibid.

Ching Chong, Chinaman: Ibid., 7.

149 *had put their faith in God*: Ibid., 132.

the negative feelings: Ibid., 48.

Don't you remember why: Ibid., 23.

the realities of life: Ibid.

150 *always the optimist*: Ibid., 54.

I don't want dirty Japs: Ibid.

151 *I felt rich*: Ibid., 67.

a feeling of great solace: Ibid., 124.

nothing spectacular but a good firm foundation: Ibid., 134.

152 *wants young people to know*: Mary Paik Lee, in Jane Iwamura and Paul Spickard, *Revealing the Sacred in Asian and Pacific America* (Abingdon-on-Thames, UK: Routledge, 2013), 319.

Aelred of Rievaulx

153 *We are constantly shedding*: Elizabeth Bernstein, "The Science of Making Friends," *Wall Street Journal,* April 18, 2016, www.wsj.com/articles/the-science-of-making-friends-1460992572.

154 *Nothing seemed to me*: Aelred of Rievaulx, *Spiritual Friendship* (Collegeville, MN: Cistercian, 1974), 45.

deceived by its mere: Ibid., 83.

155 *witty and eloquent*: Walter Daniel, *The Life of Aelred of Rievaulx* (Oxford: Clarendon, 1978), xxxiii.

156 *Such men love*: Aelred of Rievaulx, *Spiritual Friendship*, 107.

156 *a wondrous consolation*: Aelred of Rievaulx, in *The Way of Friendship: Selected Spiritual Writings*, ed. Basil Pennington (Hyde Park, NY: New City Press, 2001), 41.

Here we are: Aelred of Rievaulx, *Spiritual Friendship*, 51.

158 *as a little child*: Daniel, *Life of Aelred*, 120.

159 *no division of minds, affections, wills*: Aelred, *Spiritual Friendship*, commentary by Dennis Billy, trans. Mary Eugenia Laker, Classics with Commentary Series (Notre Dame, IN: Ave Maria Press, 2008), 84.

Love increased between: Aelred of Rievaulx, *Spiritual Friendship*, 128.

embrace of Christ: Ibid., 124.

Ignatius of Loyola

162 *given to the vanities*: Ignatius of Loyola, in George E. Ganss, *Ignatius of Loyola: The Spiritual Exercises and Selected Works* (Mahwah, NJ: Paulist Press, 1991), 68.

163 *what Saint Francis*: Ibid., 16.

without hope: Ibid., 202.

164 *the Spiritual Exercises*: Summary based on Tim Muldoon, *The Ignatian Workout: Daily Spiritual Exercises for a Healthy Faith* (Chicago: Loyola Press, 2004), xxvii.

way of proceeding: Ignatius of Loyola, in Ganss, *Ignatius of Loyola*, 256.

greatest glory to God: Ibid., 393.

166 *ad majorem*: James Martin, *My Life with the Saints* (Chicago: Loyola Press, 2006), 73.

The goal: Ignatius of Loyola, in Michael Harter, *Hearts on Fire: Praying with Jesuits* (Chicago: Loyola Press, 2005), 7.

167 *Our only desire*: Ignatius of Loyola, in David L. Fleming, *What Is Ignatian Spirituality?* (Chicago: Loyola Press, 2010), 3.

everything has the potential: Harter, *Hearts on Fire*, 8.

Juana Ines de la Cruz

170 *slay my poor mother*: Juana Ines de la Cruz, in Michelle A. Gonzalez, *Sor Juana: Beauty and Justice in the Americas* (Maryknoll, NY: Orbis, 2003), 4.

170 *I would abstain*: Ibid., 28.

171 *erudite showdown*: Jerome R. Adams, *Notable Latin American Women: Twenty-Nine Leaders, Rebels, Poets, Battlers, and Spies, 1500-1900* (Jefferson, NC: McFarland, 1995), 58.

Of all my country: Juana Ines de la Cruz, in ibid., 59.

beauties with which to stock the mind: Juana Ines de la Cruz, *A Sor Juana Anthology*, trans. Alan S. Trueblood (Cambridge, MA: Harvard University Press, 1988), 12.

172 *I took the veil*: Juana Ines de la Cruz, in Gonzalez, *Sor Juana*, 32.

only 1,200 young women are preparing: Kathleen Sprows Cummings, "Understanding U.S. Catholic Sisters Today," Foundation and Donors Interested in Catholic Activities, December 2015, www.nationalcatholic sistersweek.org/_resources/FDC_001_Report.pdf.

I do not value treasures: Juana Ines de la Cruz, in Gonzalez, *Sor Juana*, 36.

173 *inclination to study*: Juana Ines de la Cruz, in *Sor Juana Anthology*, 210.

174 *that breed arrogance*: Ibid., 200-201.

Let those things be left: Ibid., 209.

Let us rejoice: Juana Ines de la Cruz, in Gonzalez, *Sor Juana*, 57.

Grace lies not in your hand: Ibid., 71.

175 *If my intellect*: Ibid., 37.

natural impulse: Juana Ines de la Cruz, in *Sor Juana Anthology*, 210.

176 *to make a Heaven*: Juana Ines de la Cruz, in Gonzalez, *Sor Juana*, 62.

Sophie Scholl

177 *Our footsteps*: Melina Rapazzini, "El Camino del Immigrante," Project on Lived Theology blog, October 2016, www.livedtheology.org /resources/el-camino-del-immigrante.

178 *What I want*: Robert Scholl, in Donna Kafer, *Women of Faith* (Newberry, FL: Bridge Logos Foundation, 2008), 134.

179 *If those bastards harm my children*: Inge Aicher-Scholl, in Hermann Vinke, *The Short Life of Sophie Scholl*, trans. Hedwig Pachter (New York: Harper & Row, 1984), 54.

179 *No one had time for a sensible conversation*: Ibid., 45.

I will never understand: Sophie Scholl, in ibid., 71.

Braving all powers: Ibid., 94.

Isn't it a tremendous enigma: Ibid.

I will try: Sophie Scholl, in Annette Dumbach and Jud Newborn, *Sophie Scholl and the White Rose* (London: Oneworld, 2007), 19.

180 *It's high time*: Quoted in J. Kile, "Hans Scholl," MoralHeroes.org, February 28, 2014, http://moralheroes.org/hans-scholl.

181 *Finally someone has the courage*: Hans Scholl, quoted in Brenna Cussen, "The White Rose Martyrs," *Paxshalom* (blog), February 18, 2011, https://paxshalom.wordpress.com/2011/02/18/the-white-rose-martyrs.

the leaflets: Excerpted in Kathryn J. Atwood, *Women Heroes of World War II* (Chicago: Chicago Review Press, 2011), 15.

182 *I shall cling*: Sophie Scholl, in Steve Harper, *Talking in the Dark: Praying When Life Doesn't Make Sense* (Nashville: Upper Room Books, 2007), 72.

Somebody, after all, had to make a start: Quoted in Atwood, *Women Heroes*, 15.

Such a glorious, sunny day: Else Gebel, quoting Sophie Scholl in Vinke, *Short Life of Sophie Scholl*, 176.

I have no hatred: Hans Scholl, in ibid., 186.

Remember, Sophie: Magdalene Scholl, in ibid., 187.

I didn't know that dying could be so easy: Christoph Probst, in ibid., 188.

Long live freedom: Ibid.

183 *hardly a single person*: Sophie Scholl, in Ruth Hanna Sachs, *White Rose History, Volume II (Academic Version): Journey to Freedom (May 1, 1942–October 12, 1943)* (Los Angeles: Exclamation! Publishers, 2005), 6.

184 *How can we expect*: Sophie Scholl, in Inge Scholl, *The White Rose: Munich, 1942–43* (Middleton, CT: Wesleyan University Press, 2011), 56.

Conclusion

185 *The marvel*: Henri de Lubac, *The Discovery of God* (Grand Rapids: Eerdmans, 1960), 158.

186 *All of a sudden*: Ibid., 159.